2020 Year of Plenty

by Dr Afiniki Akanet

2020 Year of Plenty
by Afiniki Akanet

Second edition produced and published in May 2022
by Affinity Global Enterprises (AGE) Ltd
www.afiniki.co.uk

Paperback ISBN: 978-1-7397416-0-0
Ebook ISBN: 978-1-7397416-1-7

Printed by TJ Books Limited, Padstow, Cornwall

DEDICATION

Dedicated to everyone who will never forget 2020.

APPRECIATION

Thank you to my dear husband and two beautiful children for their support in letting me have time to write this book, and be all that God has made me to be. You three make my life so enjoyable, even on the hard days. You are truly the best!

I am also very grateful to my extended family, friends, neighbours and colleagues, who are too many to mention. I really appreciate all you do for us. Thank you also to all my patients, who teach me every day through their experiences how to be a better person and doctor. Even though this book is based on true events, some details have been changed to retain anonymity.

Greatest thanks to my God and Saviour, Jesus Christ, my Almighty Father, my eternal hope of glory, my joy and strength, my life and the length of my days. I cannot talk or write about 2020 without thanking God. I am also grateful to City Church Coventry, for being there for me and my family, through thick and thin. To the wider Ministries Without Borders, thank you for being a true community of love, expressing God's Kingdom and purpose in this world. To my childhood church, Rhema

Living Word Agape Global Ministries, thank you for being faithful in laying a good foundation and planting the good seed of God's word in our hearts.

I would also like to thank Mrs. Margaret Greenway, Dr. Chris Taggart, Ms. Trish Adudu, Mrs. Diane Rickard, Mr. Paul Sheffield and Dr. Anna Nguyen for their early reviews of this book. Your time and feedback are much appreciated. Special thanks also to my cover designer, editors and publishers, especially Jesse and Lottie, for doing a good job to make this book presentable for my precious readers. Thank you to everyone who has been part of my 2020.

I also want to genuinely thank you for reading this now. You make writing worthwhile!

FOREWORD

By Trish Adudu, 2020

There is so much to say about the year 2020. For me, it was terrible because I lost friends and had to self-isolate after testing positive for Coronavirus myself in November 2020, with no symptoms. I have family members who suffered with long Covid symptoms, and there are many people who remain traumatised by the experience of being ill and admitted with Coronavirus infection. The emotional, mental and financial impacts of lockdown have been very hard on many Coventry and Warwickshire families, who may have also lost loved ones this year. I think most people around the world will agree that 2020 has not been a great year at all.

Afiniki is not just a talented mother and medical professional, but an eternal feel-good optimist. If anyone is going to see the good in 2020, it is going to be Afiniki! Her journey and experiences of the year 2020, having to deal with everything from helping patients as a GP to juggling the challenges of buying a house have been interesting. It is mesmerising to see how she finds ways through her faith to stay strong and support her everyday decisions.

Even amongst the tough months and bad days, there were things to be grateful for, which we can trust Afiniki to point out, leaving us inspired and hopeful for the future. 2020 is a year many of us would rather forget, but may never be able to. This book offers a fresh and unique perspective of a year we might mentally just want to write off. If we ever needed a good read to help us remember the best bits of 2020 that we may have forgotten or overlooked, then this is the book to read.

Trish Adudu
BBC Radio & TV Presenter

Other books by Afiniki Akanet

- Fortitude (The Story of a Nigerian Girl in the UK)
- Felicity
- Life Without Coffee (Choosing Happiness Over Stress)
- Taking CSA Tomorrow (Get in the right mindset for your MRCGP exam)
- Money and Mental Wellbeing

All available from **Amazon.co.uk** and **Afiniki.co.uk**
Cover design by **CharlotteBlake.com**
#PsalmPlenty

Contents

INTRODUCTION..1
Chapter 1—JANUARY High Hopes...............................5
Chapter 2—FEBRUARY Business as usual...................23
Chapter 3—MARCH Lockdown begins.......................40
Chapter 4—APRIL Key Workers...................................59
Chapter 5—MAY Quarantine birthdays........................75
Chapter 6—JUNE Summer days...................................90
Chapter 7—JULY Ten years already............................108
Chapter 8—AUGUST Dream house...........................130
Chapter 9—SEPTEMBER Second wave.....................154
Chapter 10—OCTOBER Flu season..........................174
Chapter 11—NOVEMBER Lockdown Two.............197
Chapter 12—DECEMBER A Different Christmas....216
Other books by Afiniki Akanet..................................231

INTRODUCTION

The year 2020 will remain a memorable year, not just because of the Coronavirus pandemic, but also because of social restrictions and lifestyle changes people never thought possible. Coronavirus disease (Covid-19) is an infectious disease caused by the newly discovered Coronavirus from late 2019 (thought to originate in Wuhan, China). People infected with the Covid-19 virus experienced mild to moderate respiratory illness, and most recovered without special treatment. Older people and those with underlying medical conditions were found to be more likely to develop serious illness when infected, some requiring admission, intensive care and even dying. As the virus spreads mainly through droplets of saliva or discharge from the nose when an infected person coughs or sneezes, the public was advised to wear face masks and wash/sanitise hands frequently to reduce its spread.

In England, schools and businesses were closed for months, facial coverings became compulsory in many places, social gatherings and events were cancelled. The economy was seriously affected. Many parents had to homeschool their children for the first time. The government made several efforts to cushion the impact of the pandemic on businesses, organisations, families and individuals, but there were still many casualties. We grew to appreciate the British National Health Service (NHS) even more, and spent several nights clapping for healthcare workers. Key workers got some appreciation for the fact that countries cannot run smoothly without them.

There were differing opinions about the timings of lockdown and how the pandemic was handled. People groaned under the inconvenience of new restrictions, while others complained that the restrictions should have been brought in sooner. Those who had family members in hospitals struggled with worry because they were not allowed to visit relatives as usual. Some people even sadly died with no loved ones around them, during the peaks of the pandemic.

Social media and news outlets were full of Coronavirus updates (monitoring numbers of new cases and Covid-19 deaths), which led to increased fear and anxiety in many. We struggled sometimes to understand government guidelines and advice to "Stay alert and control the virus". Contracts and flights were cancelled. People were forced to get used to the comfort of their own homes and countries. The world was shaken in a way that no one expected.

In the midst of all this, there were also significant events that led to the massive Black Lives Matter campaign. People suddenly had to think about their views and attitudes to racism. Some felt the need to point out that "All lives matter", but it definitely sparked serious conversations and changes in organizations. Attention was finally coming to a deep-rooted issue of discrimination in societies and institutions. There were interesting comments from President Donald Trump of America, and an exciting election of the first black and female vice-president of America, Kamala Harris, who ran for office with president Joe Biden.

For many, it felt like one thing after another in 2020 - on the news and in our personal lives. So many loved ones lost, hospital admissions, mental breakdowns, businesses closed down, investment dilemmas, and jobs at risk. Social restrictions we never imagined changed the way we lived and related for months. The hugs and handshakes we took for granted were no longer safe. The economic and psychosocial impact of the events of 2020 remains to be seen in a post-Covid world for those who survive the pandemic. Despite all this, I want to encourage people by sharing how we got through the tough times, and I am choosing to count our blessings even in a difficult year. This is not a book about facts and figures, this is not another book full of interesting medical patient cases from a GP, but a real experience of light in the darkness, and God's strength in our weakness. I hope you enjoy my 2020 story and remember something good about your 2020 too - if you were here!

Chapter 1
JANUARY
High Hopes

A crowded airport with suited men holding up name cards to receive guests from abroad. Families travelling together. Children calling for their mothers. Lovers holding hands as they walk. Bright lights and clean floors. Colourful books and magazines in attractive airport stores. Trolleys heavy with boxes. Smartly dressed airline staff walking in groups, smiling at admiring passengers. Business people with only hand luggage. Casually dressed young people with clothes that look too skimpy for the cold weather. A 16-year-old Nigerian girl in an oversized winter coat with just one box, looking slightly lost.

She spots her name on one of the name cards held up at Arrivals, but the man was not wearing a suit like the others. He looked kind and wise, even though he was not smiling. She walks up to him and greets politely, guessing he is the driver sent to pick her up. He helps her with her box and explains that it will be a two-hour drive to her new college in Leicester. They walk away from the sights and sounds of the airport into the car park. There were so many cars in the multi-storey car park, neatly in their rows. She wondered how it could be so quiet and organised in an airport car park busier than the one she left in Nigeria. She noticed the man put some money in a machine. He explained that he was paying for parking, and they would soon be on their way.

He kindly found her a phone box a few minutes into their journey, so she could phone to tell her family that she had arrived safely in the UK. It was good to hear her mother's voice on the phone. She missed home already, but she was excited to finally be where she wanted to be. It was cold, but she liked that the roads were good and the air felt fresh. She read about top British universities and student life as a little girl, and always wanted to study abroad. There was not much to see on the motorways, so she asked the nice driver questions about Leicester. She looked forward to starting her student life in the UK with plans to become a medical doctor one day. As they approached her student accommodation, she noticed the houses on the streets all looked similar. The roads seemed quiet for a Sunday morning. Memories of heavy traffic and groups of people heading to and from church on hot Sundays in Nigeria made her start to miss home again, until she noticed the beautiful park on the other side of the street, with boys playing football.

The sound of the pilot's announcement brought me back to reality. Our flight was about to land, and my mind had drifted away to memories of my first arrival into the UK over 20 years ago. This time, I was arriving as a UK-trained medical doctor, who had just completed specialty training in General Practice (Family Medicine). I was returning as a grown woman with my own two children, and being picked up by my husband. It had been a special holiday because we attended my youngest sister's wedding, and my children spent time in their grandparents' houses. My children were very pleased to be back home to England to open their Christmas presents, which I was cruel enough to let them see, but not open until we came back after Christmas. Sometimes, waiting is good to remind ourselves and our children that Christmas is not all about the presents. Christmas is about Christ. Family. Giving. Life. Love.

I really wanted to maintain my connection to Nigeria, and give my British children a broader worldview, but this trip to Nigeria was not easy, especially because I booked the cheaper, longer flights through Dubai. We also had to finish our horrible daily malaria prevention tablets, and I surprised myself with how religiously I took those tablets while abroad this time. Maybe I was finally a real doctor, not hating medication so much. Or could it be that motherhood had reset my brain? I believe every good mother wants to give her children the best and be there for them. This is sometimes the greatest motivation for what we do, as women.

As usual, I had my plans for the new year. I decided to plan fewer parties this year. Perhaps the excitement of hosting big parties was wearing off with age. Our annual summer barbeque and charity parties gradually faded into other events, once I had birthday parties to organise for my son and daughter. Yes, I know you don't have to plan a birthday party for your children every year, but when you have a severe case of "working mum guilt", it is the bare minimum you do, because that is the only time your children get to do whatever *they* want.

My children were looking forward to their friend's birthday party on Saturday, and I also had to get the house sorted for a church meeting we were hosting that weekend. Little did we know that simple meetings like these would become almost impossible later in the year when a pandemic originating in China finally reaches Europe.

At this point, we were only being advised against non-essential travel to China because there were no Coronavirus cases in the UK yet. One of my friends shared at the church meeting how happy she was that their house move went smoothly. When they decided to move, their friends offered to buy their house, so they didn't even need estate agents. That sounded more like what I imagined a house move to be, unlike the horror stories circulated about how moving house can be as stressful as a divorce! I had no idea how big a deal moving house was, until we decided to sell our house later in the year.

For now, we were still loving our dormer bungalow in our lovely Warwickshire village. I was also looking forward to starting my new job as a General Practitioner (GP or family doctor). Sometimes, to help my confidence, I had to remind myself that being a newly qualified GP was not the same as being a newly qualified doctor. Thanks to part-time working and maternity leave during my GP training, I had already been working as a medical doctor in the UK for seven years. I had passed my professional examinations for GP specialty training and jumped all the final hoops to allow me to add more letters after my name, dress less like a maid and more like a boss, in my very own doctor's office. Those years of no fancy rings, no wristwatches and no high heels in hospital jobs as a junior doctor were truly character-building for a woman like me. With respect to my hospital colleagues, I would like to say that I sometimes miss my days of running around as a junior doctor in hospitals, but that would be lying.

God made us all different, and I am so glad some people love working in hospitals, so we do not all have to do it. I did enjoy doing home visits as a GP registrar though, so I planned to sign up for some Out of Hours work, visiting patients at the weekends. There is something interesting about seeing a patient in their own home and having a glimpse into their everyday life and problems, from *their* perspective. I guess I was always meant to be a GP, not a hospital doctor. I still enjoy getting to know patients and providing continuity of care in the community, which is why I accepted a Monday to Friday job at a local GP practice.

One of my big plans for 2020 was to start a Yoruba language class (called Wazobia classes) at our village hall to help raise money for charity, while teaching local children a Nigerian language. My children speak very well, with an impressive English accent, which sometimes makes me sorely aware of my Nigerian immigrant status. My daughter and son, at almost ages six and four, sometimes speak like adults. I knew it was time to do something when they started making fun of other languages and asking why my mother was "talking funny", whenever she spoke to me in Hausa. Thankfully, we were able to get some wonderful Yoruba-speaking volunteers to teach the classes on Sunday afternoons, because I do not speak Yoruba myself, and my dear Yoruba husband had warned me that he is not a teacher. We had a good number of families attending our Yoruba classes regularly from Coventry and Warwickshire, so my children learned a lot and enjoyed it.

Part of the job of organising the language classes for Forte Charity was advertising it on social media pages and forums. I had to include a phone number for parents to contact for more information.

"Hello, are you the one running the Wazobia language classes?"

"Yes, we meet on Sundays, 3pm - 4pm at the village hall."

"My children are seven and nine. We have been struggling to teach them Yoruba, even though my wife and I are Nigerian Yorubas. I just wanted to find out more about it."

"Of course, we would love to have them there on Sundays. We have children from age one up to 12, and the volunteers are mostly experienced school teachers. They have been great at engaging the children and teaching them easy lessons so far, like counting and greeting in Yoruba. The children also enjoy meeting up with other Black-British children to learn more about Nigerian culture. It is only £2 per child each week, which is actually a donation to Forte Charity"

"Hmm, so the class is for one hour?"

"Yes, they do have a short break within the hour, and we do some Yoruba singing too. We also give them sheets with the new words learned to take home."

"So what can I expect by the end of the year, will they be able to speak Yoruba fluently?"

"*Sure! For only £2 a week, we can teach them in less than 50 hours what you have been unable to do for seven years. We will also make sure they can write Yoruba novels and speak proverbs like the elders. We also plan to teach Maths and English for the same fee on Saturdays, so parents paying £20,000 a year at private schools can save some money by coming to us instead.*"

This is just one of the lovely phone conversations I got to have in January, but I did not actually say the last bit - as much as I wanted to! Most parents who brought their children to our Sunday classes were just grateful for the opportunity to get their children interested in learning Yoruba and mixing with other like-minded families, while raising money for the charity's educational projects in African countries. We had some non-Nigerian supporters of the charity coming to learn Yoruba too, which was great. There was a lot of supporting material on Youtube, and those who spoke Yoruba with their children at home during the week got more out of it, as expected. My own children had no chance, with a mother who speaks almost no Yoruba and a Yoruba father who now breathes in English.

We got exciting news about winning an International Changemakers travel grant for travel to Lagos, as part of the Coventry City of Culture 2021 plans. I planned to go with another Forte Charity trustee, who is also a good friend and GP trainee. Flight tickets were booked for the May school holiday week, and I bought tickets for my children to come along. At this point, no one could have imagined that the developing pandemic would change our travel plans so drastically.

I was enjoying my new GP job, but it took a few weeks to get used to the new computer software at the practice. I had a tiny office in the old building we were using, while a purpose-built surgery was being put up. What mattered most to me was that I had a good relationship with my colleagues and most of the patients. As all GPs know, there will always be "difficult patients" who make you have to remind yourself why you chose the profession. I am thankful that most of my patients are sensible, polite, and sometimes even grateful. Things were a bit more difficult in my first few months at this GP practice because many of the patients were on high-dose opioids for pain control due to previous prescribing practises that were now being improved, with a more stable set of clinicians to follow up. Knowing how addictive these drugs can be, you can imagine the resistance, and sometimes verbal abuse we got whenever we suggested reducing patients' opioid doses and trying less addictive pain management options. I was so grateful that I chose to work only mornings most days, so I would not burn out too early in my career. It meant a lower salary for fewer sessions, but I also had time for my writing and some errands before picking up my children from school.

The cold weather was beginning to bite, but I had enough projects and socialising in my diary to make the days fly by. It seemed like we attended children's birthday parties almost every weekend. I even started buying items for children's birthday presents in bulk, because some weekends were too busy for a supermarket stopover before getting to the party, and I did not want to be the mum always turning up late, and without a present! My husband is also Nigerian-British and would rather be early than late. In fact, he loves keeping to time, even for casual meetings. Unlike him, I like to do one million things in my spare ten minutes, even if it means getting somewhere five minutes late - with massive apologies, of course. This means that I can sort of accept a late-comer reputation, as long as no one calls it "African time".

We did not realise how busy and full our days actually were, until the pandemic shut down places and we were forced to slow down. I remember fitting in a trip to the dry cleaners, supermarket and gym in the 90 minutes I usually have on my own before picking up my children. When you don't have to wear masks everywhere, keep your distance or wait outside the shop to go in one at a time, this is possible. There were no restrictions on how many cans of chopped tomatoes you could buy, and people did not have to wipe down every surface touched before the next customer came. We never really knew the freedom we had when we had it. I hope we appreciate it when we have it again. My visits to the gym were usually for a quick walk on the treadmill, once in a while, especially after having too much dessert. Surely, there must be other ways to get rid of this extra Christmas weight and keep fit. I soon cancelled my gym membership when I realised it would be better to bin some cash every month than to continue with this very casual, expensive relationship with the gym.

Talking about making good use of my time, I finally got round to interviewing some students in Nigeria by phone for Forte Charity grants for tuition fees. Supporting young people to get the qualifications they need to build a better life is a worthwhile cause. We use the money raised by the charity to support students who would otherwise drop out of university, but we have to make sure that the applications are genuine, with confirmation of student status from administrators at universities where we have contacts. We have had many hard-working candidates and graduates over the years, and I am yet to meet one of the shameless scammers who have given Nigeria a bad reputation to some.

Even though I like to use every hour intentionally, I have learned over time to hold plans loosely because God sometimes has a detour planned. Some people believe in mother nature, the universe, other or no higher power, but I believe in God. I remember leaving work early after my morning GP session one day because the computers crashed and would not let me do other administrative work. I decided to run some important errands before school closed, but was surprised to see traffic building up in front of the hospital I normally drive past to work. It is a hospital dear to my heart because of my years of training there, even more now that it had the words "Thank you NHS" marked on the road to the hospital. There was a psychiatric inpatient unit nearby, which I had also worked in.

That morning, I could see a young girl standing in the middle of the main road, and a woman who seemed to be trying to call her away. It was hard to see people's faces properly, but there was tension in the air as impatient drivers tried to stop themselves from using their car horns, and curious ones kept rubbernecking. I felt God ask me to stop and help. From a distance, it just looked like people being silly on the road. With my psychiatry experience, it looked like a mental health patient being difficult for her support worker, who would soon get help from trained staff in the nearby hospital. I am not the type who enjoys getting involved in emergencies, and this was not the plan for today, but "Nokay", I said to God, like my little son says when he obeys us reluctantly. No + okay.

I found a side road to park safely and realized when I walked back to the main road that the young girl was actually suicidal. The support worker had been phoning for help, but felt out of her depth now while waiting. She was so grateful I stopped, and I was glad I could be an answer to someone's prayer on her bad day at work. The patient started listening to me when I introduced myself as a doctor, so I started assessing her level of intent versus protective factors. I was able to keep her distracted by talking about her brother who might miss her. We were still standing in the middle of the road because she did not move much, but we were only blocking one lane now. She was only a teenager, but twice my size, so there was no way I could physically stop her if she got violent. My hairs stood on their ends with heart racing as her countenance changed and she started to make sudden movements, but I continued to speak calmly and prayed in my heart. God never sends us out alone, because He is our ever-present help. I was sad to see a young girl feeling so hopeless and unwell. The police came just in time to get her off the road a few minutes later, and no one got hurt. As they often say in Nigeria, while there is life, there is hope. I prayed she would get well soon and enjoy a full life.

Morning routines before school had become smoother in our house after a few weeks of resumption, I even managed to go into the local BBC studio one morning before work for a radio interview, to raise awareness about the charity and our Yoruba language classes. No, I did not just stroll in there. I had an appointment, and I was on time! I always enjoy opportunities to talk about my work as a GP and charity trustee. I never imagined that such face-to-face interviews would be almost impossible in the Zoom age to come. Zoom is a software application people used a lot for video conference calls in 2020, in case it is gone by the time you read this. I even had to do one such radio interview some months later in my parked car at a supermarket (with my children in the back seats). The oversubscribed internet could not support a smooth wifi phone call at my house, because many people had to work from home in the pandemic. The internet companies must have had to do a lot of upgrading, because connections got better eventually in 2021.

I tried to remain keen on attending optional lectures for GPs on Wednesday afternoons. It was a good opportunity to see old friends and network, get updates about current medical guidelines and hear from hospital specialists. The free lunch was also an incentive when I was younger, but somehow the food was not as impressive this year. There were usually around 100 GPs, and I sat next to my friend who had just written one of our professional exams. She had also just completed a Masters degree during a year out of GP training, and had one more GP exam to take before becoming fully qualified. Some of the most amazing and hard-working doctors I knew were in that room. We had no idea such large meetings would soon be impossible because of the developing pandemic. Well, maybe the cleverest ones of us knew.

I always looked forward to the weekends, not because I hate work, but because we usually got to visit or host friends. As I am not good at phoning friends regularly, we try to plan visits to see people in different cities for a proper catch-up and change in scenery. This weekend included a trip to Liverpool to see university friends and old friends from the church we attended as students. I was sad to hear that one of my uncles in Liverpool was ill in hospital, so we went to visit him. I had no idea how seriously ill he was before that day, but it was a blessing to be able to pray with him and his wife. My fondest memory of him is of the first time I brought my university boyfriend (who is now my husband) to meet him. Uncle could just never remember my boyfriend's name during that visit. My husband was worried my uncle did not like him, but I found it funny because I think boyfriends sometimes need to be kept on their toes. My husband grew to relax around them with time, as my uncle and his wife were always so loving and welcoming to us both after our wedding.

Normally, people complain about January being the longest month, after all the Christmas expenses and events, but this one went fast for me with all the changes. It was nice to now be earning as a qualified GP and working the hours I chose. I have always said that the best thing about good pay rates has to be the option to work fewer hours. I was so grateful to be able to enjoy working every day, while still having time to do other things I wanted to do. There were now two confirmed Coronavirus cases in the UK, but we had no idea how soon things would escalate. The regular income from my permanent part-time job turned out to be a big blessing to my family in the months to come when optional GP locum work dried up. This was never my first choice job from a distance, but as soon as I went for the interview in 2019 as a GP trainee, I knew this GP practice was where I was meant to be for my first GP job. It was not just a job for money, but a place for me to grow and be a blessing to others. In December 2019, we heard in church (both in England and Nigeria, interestingly) how God was saying that 2020 would be a year of plenty, and I believed it.

Hebrews 11:1 (Holy Bible)
Now faith is the substance of things hoped for,
the evidence of things not seen.

Chapter 2
FEBRUARY
Business as usual

My children's six-monthly dental check-up was scheduled for this month. This is something I try to take them regularly for, especially while it is free for children in England. We had no idea how precious dental services would become later in 2020 when dentists were understandably seeing only patients with dental emergencies, because of Covid-19 infection risk. I remember getting a shocking bill from the dentist when I had to get my broken tooth filling sorted privately in the summer. I almost asked them to take the filling back out, before I remembered the delicious plantain crisps in my car which I had not been able to eat all week, and grudgingly paid their receptionist. Thank God for subsidised NHS treatments and medical services that are free at the point of delivery. People in some countries have to wait for years to get free surgery from charities like Mercy Ships. At work, we had patients calling to request antibiotics from GPs, because they could not get dental appointments in the pandemic, but I am sure dentists will have stories to tell also about patients complaining about lack of enough GP appointments. Dental health is something else I was very grateful for in 2020.

My children just love going out, even to the dentist. My daughter was so pleased to hear that her teeth were healthy. My son did not seem to care what the dentist said, as long as I paid up on whatever bribe I promised for good behaviour at the dental surgery. Sometimes, it does come down to bribery for a quieter life. I always feel sorry for mums that try hard to show what good parents they are in public with some PDD - Public Display of Discipline. Surely any child would be much better behaved if they truly heard all that preaching at home already, every day, before today - but who am I to judge? Maybe other children just don't like sweets as much as mine do.

It was soon another "hair weekend", as I call it. Mummy versus the Afro. I did pray for my daughter to have lovely long hair, but I must have forgotten how interesting it is looking after Afro hair. These days, we spend almost one hour taking out the plaits. This has to be done slowly for minimal tears, then comb it while wet (because I finally learned it is better to comb it while washing), then condition and blow dry very gently to avoid more whining, before plaiting it again - with less patience than before, because Mummy is already fed up at this point. I do try to empathise when I remember how tough it was having tight curls before I straightened my hair. It is just that we did not get that much sympathy as little girls while getting our hair done in Nigeria, because everyone else had the same Afro hair and just learned to get on with it.

I have since met many black women who are Afro experts and have kindly offered me helpful products for styling my daughter's beautiful hair, but for me, there is still the issue of precious time spent sorting it, which I choose to look upon now as mother-daughter bonding time. We usually watch a nice movie on hair days and talk about everything.

"Mummy, what is shagging?"

"Hmm, where did you hear that, darling?" I replied calmly.

"On TV. Kyla said she had a shaggy dog."

"Oooh, shaggy." Phew! I was so glad I did not jump into explaining the wisdom of saving sex for marriage to a five-year-old. I must remember to always check before answering in future, and maybe get my own mind out of the gutter!

In spite of what I sometimes thought was a traumatic experience for her with my impatient hair-styling techniques, my daughter would choose me over a professional hairdresser any day. I realised that I probably, secretly, subconsciously, surprisingly, like doing her hair too. When she asked to cut her hair short like mine in the summer, my answer was "No, please!"

Weekends for us sometimes also included a trip to Stratford-upon-Avon, because of my daughter's violin lessons there. Stratford is Shakespeare's birthplace, and one of my favourite English towns. I hoped to live there one day. We always enjoyed our short trips to Stratford, looking at the lovely scenery and houses. The houses there cost more than those in our village, and I could understand why. Some of my favourite babysitting clients were from Stratford, when I still had my babysitting agency, Evasitters. The events of 2020 made me grateful I had closed down Evasitters last year before all this. My babysitting staff would definitely not have been able to work with Covid-19 social distancing restrictions. I would have been so worried about their lack of income when they were not working, and worried about their Covid-19 exposure when they were working. I would have still had regular business expenses and paperwork, which I was glad I did not have to worry about while homeschooling. Closing down the business has also allowed me to really enjoy GP work and time with my family this year. After five years of Evasitters, I had learned a lot about what kind of business Mum I did not want to become, so that was definitely a "God decision". My heart really went out to struggling businesses and entrepreneurs in 2020, but one thing I know for sure is that even the "failed" business ventures and "unlucky" moments add up to a great success story when we give it all to God, and trust that He will work things out for our good.

My children both enjoy music. The girl was inspired to learn to play the violin after seeing an amazing young player on Youtube. I had to learn a little of the basics to help my daughter practice, but it did not take long for her to start playing independently. Now, we just take her to lessons and watch as she speaks musical mysteries with her tutor. Unlike her, my mind is so full of everything else, I cannot even remember which string is which now. I am always so amazed at how much children's brains develop and retain when learning music. My amazing daughter has already inspired many other children around her to start learning to play musical instruments too. I hope she continues to enjoy it.

There was growing concern as Covid-19 infection rates kept rising. There were around 20 confirmed cases in the UK this month. People were asking what I thought, whether it would lead to a lockdown here, or if it would stop abroad. A lockdown would mean the closure of offices, schools, shops etc, requiring people to stay at home for a period, to reduce the spread of the virus. As a positive person, I like to take one day at a time. At this point, we understood that Covid-19 was a virus that affected people differently. Older people and those with other risk factors and serious health conditions seemed to suffer more and possibly die of the infection, but it could also cause only mild symptoms or none in others. There were no robust Covid-19 testing services and scientists were still researching treatments and vaccines. It was anybody's guess how it would go, so we just hoped for the best and carried on with life. My son was still going to nursery, which I was so thankful for, as GP work got busier.

Reliable childcare from 8am to 6pm will never be taken for granted after 2020. It was so nice that my son could have three healthy meals on weekdays at nursery, so I did not have to worry about cooking something less spicy every night for dinner. Somehow, the boy just could not tolerate spicy Nigerian food, but he does love his food! He could eat a horse after three meals at nursery, if you let him. After Covid-19 restrictions started, our nursery had a later opening time to allow for deep cleaning in the mornings, so we had to give our children breakfast at home. Let's just say we spent a small fortune on breakfast cereals. Grandparents could no longer help with childcare due to shielding. The government advised vulnerable and elderly people to shield during lockdown by staying indoors for weeks and avoiding contact with anyone outside their household to reduce risk of infection. Many holiday clubs were also closed. We used to complain about childcare being expensive, but after a few weeks of being stuck at home with our own children, and no help from relatives, many parents would gladly pay double.

We got a greater appreciation in 2020 for the contribution of grandparents (through childcare) to allow young parents to go to work. People were phoning doctors complaining about feeling depressed about not seeing their grandchildren for six weeks, and I sometimes wondered if they knew that many of our children had not seen their grandparents abroad for over six months. I guess things were not as bad for us because our children were already used to having video calls with their grandparents instead of regular hugs, so this was not a big change. I realised later though that hearing people complain about something you have learned to get used to can sometimes make you feel very sorry for yourself. As first-generation immigrants, we were used to paying for childcare, so we had no family childcare to miss. I used to dream of how wealthy we would become in September when our son could start state school and have no more private nursery fees to pay. Then I remembered music lessons, after school clubs, sports clubs, swimming lessons, community clubs, school trips etc etc, and got back to work.

The main "commercial event" of February is Valentine's Day. The shops were full of cards and gifts, reminding us to spend. After nine years of marriage, I do not really remember what we did on Valentine's Day, but it was romantic. I am sure I would have remembered clearly if my husband forgot. I was impressed with how British I have become though, when I smiled nicely at a lovely little boy bringing cards and chocolates for my five-year-old daughter on Valentine's Day. If this happened when I was a little girl in Nigeria, both of us children would have had enough telling off to make us forget about love and marriage for another 50 years!

Sometimes, I think children these days have it so easy. My children begged us for pet chickens and finally got some over a year ago. We had the fantastic idea that having the chickens would help them learn responsibility when they have to feed them every day. It was all good at first with the children keenly going out with their father in the mornings to feed the chickens. Now, the children only remember to play with the chickens once in a while, and my dear husband has to feed them himself, in all weathers, every morning. I was glad I made it clear from the beginning that I did not want chickens or any related outdoor work. The chickens did earn their keep by providing eggs for us in lockdown shortages though, so I bonded with them a bit then. I can only imagine what would have happened if I abandoned any of my chores for my Dad when growing up. I might have ended up living in the garden with the chickens!

Mealtimes are always interesting at our home because our children have so much to say. My husband sometimes cooks on the weekend, and we try to encourage the children to set the table when they want to be helpful, considering I do most of this on weekdays. This time, the boy was helping his dad in the kitchen, while I sorted the laundry.

"Please remember to put out the cutlery, Buddy."

"Yes, Daddy. Are we eating dead fish? Mummy does not like dead fish."

"I know, there is other meat for her. Your sister likes fish. Doesn't she?"

"Yes, but we haven't had dead fish in a long time."

"Fish is nice, we just don't eat it often because of Mummy. Where is your sister?"

"In the lounge. Maybe we can have ketchup with the dead fish?"

"Stop calling it '*dead* fish'!"

At this, I had to burst out laughing. He never says dead chicken for cooked chicken, but I guess the boy was trying to make a distinction between the fish he was about to eat and the goldfish in our aquarium.

There was more conversation about my daughter's new "shark teeth" at the dinner table. I later found out that it is quite common for children to have new teeth behind the baby teeth, and dentists advised parents to let the new teeth grow and push out the baby teeth eventually. I really hoped they were right, because I am not convinced sharks and humans are meant to cohabit.

I finally managed to book a graduation gown and photos online for my upcoming GP Royal College ceremony. After missing my first-degree graduation, I was excited to get to have another graduation after the one for medical school. This was going to be the celebration of a lifelong dream, which seemed almost impossible twelve years ago when I had to take a year out of medical school due to financial difficulties. I remember how I used to stay up late with my husband talking about my desire to become a GP and how he wanted to own a healthcare business one day. The year 2020, with all else it brought, also brought some answered prayers for us. One of my lovely GP friends planned to go for the ceremony on the same day next month, so we arranged to meet there with our families.

I enjoyed my freedom to visit people this month, with spontaneous child-free visits to our neighbours when I had a spare hour before picking up the children. It is sometimes difficult to have a proper adult conversation with my daughter trying to tell people about her new books and my boy asking questions about everything. Not to mention the way my heart skips when they keep reaching out to touch people's expensive home decor. I am pleased that my children love reading and asking questions, but I am also glad that they have teachers to do that with for most of the day. My son's favourite question to ask people in 2020 was, "Do you know Jesus?"

We also visited family in Hertfordshire without worrying about the 'Rule of six', which I am hoping will be a distant memory by the time you read this. Coronavirus social restrictions later this year meant that a maximum of only six people including children were allowed to meet indoors in England, so we could not visit other families anymore. People with three or four children were upset about not being able to see grandparents or couples. It was sometimes tricky understanding the rules for outdoor and indoor meetings, so I just stopped trying to physically meet up with people at some point. The temptation to hug old friends when we met was too much, and I did not want to be the one shamelessly breaking rules all the time. I learned to use my phone more and thanked God for the blessing of the internet.

One of the meetings I attended this month was a bursary meeting for winners of the City of Culture International Changemakers award. I went with another Forte Charity trustee to explain what we planned to do in Lagos. We met some lovely journalists, charity workers and local professionals there. Who would have thought a meeting of 50 people would be impossible in only a few months? Coronavirus social distancing restrictions meant that many weddings were cancelled or postponed. Imagine a bride's frustration after months of careful preparation and planning. Wedding vendors such as photographers and caterers lost income, and had to find other jobs while supporting disappointed clients. Thankfully, funerals and weddings were later allowed to be held, with less than 30 people present. I think that would have been better than nothing, but you can just imagine the conversations among families when you have to cut down an African wedding guest list from 500 to 30!

As doctors' learning never ends, I was also working on an audit at work, which meant going through several patients' notes to gather information about the care they were getting. We usually present the findings from such audits to our practice staff to see how we can improve our services. Work was going well, I even managed to do a few enjoyable locum sessions at other surgeries this month. Even though it sometimes feels like a pain to have to keep learning after university and exams, I think it is great when we can fit reading around other aspects of life. I try to encourage our children to enjoy reading too, so we visit the local library regularly for books to keep them entertained while I do my writing or reading. There was also entertainment for school holidays to be sorted, so I keenly booked summer holiday clubs for my children in advance this month, because my boy was finally old enough to attend with his school-aged sister.

My son was due to start school in September. We were not planning to have any more children, and it felt good to be a more mature family, with no nappies or nursery. My husband mentioned this month that he was also now beginning to feel that it is time for us to move on from our house into something bigger, as the children got older. Since I had already felt this way for months, that was all the motivation I needed to sign up for Rightmove alerts. There are several websites for buying and selling houses, but Rightmove was the most popular in our area. Knowing how proactive I am, I'm sure my husband was not surprised to hear that I booked house viewings for us a few days later. Our house hunting system in the past had been for me to view houses, make a shortlist and then take him to see the ones I liked, so we could make a decision. I was so excited because this could be my chance to finally live in Stratford since it was close to my husband's next job. We were in the early stages of buying over a healthcare business in Warwickshire, where he hoped to work once we had NHS England approval to take over. We applied for this a few weeks before now and hoped that the pandemic would not delay things too much. Even though I was not keen on driving, I liked Stratford enough to not mind driving a bit farther from there to my current GP job when we eventually got a house and business near there.

It all sounded like a good plan, even though my phone was still being bombarded with Covid-19 news. The World Health Organisation had already labelled the Coronavirus outbreak a Public Health Emergency of International Concern. GPs unsurprisingly had more Covid-19 information coming to them than the general public. I hoped somehow that the pandemic would not affect our little plans. Rumours of a possible lockdown kept going around. I was not sure what that would really mean for us if it happened. There was so much uncertainty in the air, but we were encouraged in church on Sunday when God reminded us of Psalm 91 from the Bible, so that even when the news seemed bad, our confidence was in God.

Psalm 91

Whoever dwells in the shelter of the Most High
  will rest in the shadow of the Almighty.
I will say of the Lord, "He is my refuge and my fortress,
  my God, in whom I trust."
Surely he will save you
  from the fowler's snare

and from the deadly pestilence.
He will cover you with his feathers,
and under his wings you will find refuge;
his faithfulness will be your shield and rampart.
You will not fear the terror of night,
nor the arrow that flies by day,
nor the pestilence that stalks in the darkness,
nor the plague that destroys at midday.
A thousand may fall at your side,
ten thousand at your right hand,
but it will not come near you.
You will only observe with your eyes
and see the punishment of the wicked.
If you say, "The Lord is my refuge,"
and you make the Most High your dwelling,
no harm will overtake you,
no disaster will come near your tent.
For he will command his angels concerning you
to guard you in all your ways;
they will lift you up in their hands,
so that you will not strike your foot against a stone.
You will tread on the lion and the cobra;
you will trample the great lion and the serpent.
"Because he loves me," says the Lord, "I will rescue him;
I will protect him, for he acknowledges my name.
He will call on me, and I will answer him;

I will be with him in trouble,
I will deliver him and honor him.
With long life I will satisfy him
and show him my salvation."

I am always so grateful for God's promises and amazed by His power and love for us. I know my whole life would be completely different (in a very bad way) if I had not chosen to give my life to Jesus over 30 years ago. I have enjoyed His grace and mercy in every area. This new and eternal life is a free gift to all of mankind, which I am glad I accepted. Although God promises to take care of us, even in a pandemic, I am also aware that He expects us to live responsibly in faith. I had been meaning to lose some excess Christmas weight, but it was just not happening. I signed up to join some ladies on Monday nights for netball, which I had never played before, but every Monday, there just seemed to be no time for this. The gym was sounding like a good idea again, but I suspected there would still be no time for that too now that I had started house hunting. My children love swimming and would make sure we go, so I bought the most body-covering swimsuit and registered to use the swimming pool at a nearby hotel with my children every week so I could get some exercise. I did not realise I was getting fit for sitting at home in lockdown.

Chapter 3
MARCH
Lockdown begins

The first house I viewed in Stratford was definitely not the one for us. I could not wait to come back to my own house. I hate it when online advertising photos are much better than the actual house. The kitchen was much older than I expected, but the main thing that put me off was the fact that I could hear and see cars on the main road from the house. The house was the last one on a close, but it was awkwardly close to a busy road on the other side, which I did not think would be safe for my small children. I politely carried on looking at the whole house with the agent, while the owners watched TV and barely looked at us. I later understood this to be the "indifference stage" of house selling, when you literally do not care anymore. This viewing made me grateful that we all have different tastes for houses, because the things that put me off would probably be the exact reason someone else wanted to buy it.

Maybe I had been spoiled having a house in a nice, quiet neighbourhood near the woods, but I knew I definitely did not want a house too close to busy roads, so there was no need to bring my husband to see this one. The first few viewings helped me to get to know which specific areas of Stratford we prefer. I carried on with my online search on Rightmove and set up alerts for the kind of houses we might like. With children that love music and the shouting that sometimes happens in our house, it was reasonable to go for a detached house again. I enjoyed renovating our dormer bungalow into a lovely modern family home, but this time I wanted a "proper house" on two floors, but not a townhouse on three floors. Having a good heavenly Father has taught me to be specific in my prayers, while trusting that He will provide what is best for us. I know that bigger is not always better, so I made a mental list of all the important things we wanted the new house to have, so that we would not regret moving. My husband thought it was funny when I said that I missed high walls and being able to hang up more photos. Thankfully, our financial adviser agreed that we could afford a detached house in Stratford. I knew it would definitely be smaller than a house in nearby Coventry for the same price, but I was happy to compromise on size for leafy Warwickshire living.

My husband worked out the numbers and gave me a maximum reasonable budget for us, which we agreed to be nowhere near the maximum mortgage we could get, because we did not want to saddle ourselves with a huge monthly repayment and a poor quality of life. When professionals talk about burnout sometimes, I wonder if it is because expenses rise to meet income, and desires rise to meet potential income, leading to hefty mortgages, expensive holidays and flashy cars to keep up appearances, to the point that people have to work all the time to pay for these things and end up hating the life they have created for themselves. Stratford also has a good choice of comprehensive, grammar and private schools, so it seemed reasonable to move there, in case I later decided to spend all the money people think GPs have on posh private schools and Ferraris. Seriously though, our little village did not have any secondary schools, and we felt that moving to an area with a greater choice of local primary and secondary schools would be easier now than when our children were older and more attached to their friends.

The next house I went to view in Stratford was on a newer estate. We are not normally keen on new-build homes because of the smaller rooms and exorbitant prices, in my opinion. I guess the price is worth it, if you really hate the hassle of renovations. I enjoyed project-managing the renovation of our current house and liked using some of the money made to pay off our huge student debts, so I definitely saw the wisdom in avoiding overpriced houses, but this one had to be seen. It was not too recently built, so I felt there was room for improvement to increase the value. After days of dreaming about how I would furnish this lovely new place, it took my husband only ten minutes to burst that bubble when we went to see it together. He immediately noticed that there was no real driveway, even though they cleverly designed it for parking space. I soon realised it was really not a good investment, when I stopped dreaming and considered the other valid points he made. It was annoying, but he was right. It was back to Rightmove for me again after I accepted that "two are better than one" and maybe four eyes are better than two.

My car's annual check-up (MOT) reminder came up on my phone diary. I could not believe it had been one year since I bought this second-hand car. When you choose to buy used cars, you have to be grateful for every good year you get, because you never really know what you are getting, even with a car dealer warranty. We have been blessed with reliable cars over the years, but have heard some horror stories of people spending so much on problematic used cars. We are realistic about what to expect with used cars, and thankfully only had a few inexpensive issues to fix since buying ours. I drove my old Ford for years and bashed it so badly with my bad parking skills.

When I decided to get a new car last year, I told my husband it would be nice to get a Peugeot again, because I enjoyed driving that before. For months, I was eyeing up every Peugeot 3008 that drove past me, while remembering my limited budget. God reminded me this week about how He provided this better Mercedes car with parking sensors when all I wanted was a Peugeot, and how He would provide the right house for us at the right time, if I just trust Him. I know Mercedes Benz is not everyone's cup of tea, but my father always said "There are two types of cars - Mercedes and others". I have not quite impressed him yet, because I ended up buying the Mercedes model reviewed as "The one wealthy people buy for their nannies to drop off their children with"!

I had my car checked at the weekend and made time for my daughter's Afro again. There is a lot of house cleaning to do when you have children, and we managed it for years with no cleaner. My husband is very helpful, but there are some things that would just be left undone if Mummy did not do them. I sometimes had "cleaner envy" when my GP friends talked about their amazing cleaners and not having to worry about this. The one time we tried to hire a cleaner, she never turned up! We decided to carry on as we were, with everyone chipping in. Even my little children know how to tidy up after themselves (with plenty of prompting), but it all came in handy later this year when no one was allowed to have visitors or cleaners. I'm not jealous at all, but the world somehow seemed fairer when everyone had to deal with their own mess.

The downside of having no cleaner is that you sometimes go into crazy Mum mode, where you just bark orders to get everything done in time for bedtime. It would be nice to just sit and play with the children because all the cleaning had been done by professionals, who would usually do a better job. I was definitely going to try getting regular cleaners for the new house, which kind of signified the start of a new phase of life for me. In the meantime, I will just carry on being robo-mum, while my husband remains their "cool buddy".

My family must think I have constipation this month though, because I keep hiding in the toilet for hours, checking out houses on Rightmove on my phone. I learned more about the new housing estate where the last house viewing was, and was excited about how warm the community seemed. It reminded me of our little village, which we did not want to miss too much when we moved. There was a local school, church and health centre. They even had a Facebook page for residents. I was not crazy enough to join the Facebook group, but I planned to drive around Stratford for an idea of which parts might have the kind of house we were after. I also got an appointment to look around the local school there, and booked estate agents to value our own house for sale, because I heard that any offers we made would not be taken seriously until our house was officially on the market.

My week was going well with the usual routines and house hunting research, until I got an email from our Practice Manager telling me that a patient had lodged a complaint with NHS England about me. I remembered who he was as soon as I saw his name. He was taken off our practice list after he became verbally aggressive towards me and a few other members of staff when I politely refused to issue some addictive medications he asked for, explaining that it was unsafe with his history and current infection. I was sad to hear that he felt the need to put in a complaint after reflecting on the incident, in which I got the abuse. It took me almost an hour to go through his medical notes and write a detailed response for NHS England, but I spent more hours reflecting on this consultation and complaint.

Everyone expects the first year of any profession to be hard, but I did not expect a complaint so early. Other GPs reassured me with the fact that most good doctors get a patient complaint every year, but somehow that made me more annoyed that some people did not appreciate good GPs. I did not have to complain about his behaviour because other doctors and the Practice Manager (who took him off our practice list, as per the zero-tolerance policy for staff abuse) could hear his loud swearing from my office, so this was probably his own way of getting back at us. I do believe it is worth having a complaints procedure so that patients have a voice and doctors are held accountable since no one is perfect, but it can be stressful to get a complaint, especially when you have gone out of your way to do what is right for the patient. It would have been a quicker consultation to just issue the requested medication. After sleeping on it, I was less upset and realised that one or two complaints a year was reasonable, because it meant that the other >99.9% of our patients were not dissatisfied with our work. I would just have to consider this part of my GP experience and learn from the outcome.

Coronavirus cases had risen to over 200 in the UK and the first Covid-19 UK death was confirmed. Glastonbury festival was cancelled, and filmings of popular BBC TV series were suspended as the number of cases rapidly rose to over 1000 this month. The news was getting scarier from abroad and at home. My email inbox was being bombarded with updates and advice for professionals and patients. Covid-19 did not seem so similar to the flu anymore. Even optimistic people like me were beginning to get more concerned. As healthcare workers, there was so much to discuss at dinner time in our house after busy days at work. My husband decided to start wearing face masks at work long before it was mandatory, because he could not afford to take long periods of time off work as a self-employed contractor. He also had an underlying medical condition which meant that he was vulnerable to severe illness if he got infected, so this was a concern to be discussed with his doctor as he really wanted to keep working. We both knew work was not just about the money for him. It was also for his mental health. He has massive respect for stay-at-home parents, but has always told me that he could not survive being a stay-at-home Dad. This was even before our children had the ability to chew off your ears!

I went to see four primary schools in Stratford this month, but sadly, the one in the new estate I liked did not make the cut. That was the deal-breaker for me. We already had a few more house viewings in that new estate, and I enjoyed seeing the lovely houses, but no matter how nice a house was, if the school in the catchment area did not feel right for my children, I would not consider buying it. Thankfully, I loved one of the four schools I visited, and had a viewing coming up for a house nearby. It was scheduled for a Saturday, when I could go with the whole family. I saw a few more houses in Stratford on weekdays with my children, but none of them felt right for us. My children just liked any house that had lovely kids' rooms, and my son really wanted space to play drums. I wanted a house with a good-sized garden, so we could hopefully get a sound-proof drumming shed for him and save our ears.

Concerns about the Coronavirus pandemic got more worrying when exams, including the GP professional exams for this month, got cancelled. I can only imagine the pain of not sitting an exam you prepared and sacrificed months for. Not to mention the follow-on impact of not taking the exams and completing training as scheduled. Families and individuals showed incredible resilience this year in changing plans and coping with unexpected hurdles. In the midst of the chaos, we got a valuation of our house from three estate agents, and it was being valued at significantly less than the latest bank valuation, in the current climate. We decided to put our house on the market anyway and signed up with an estate agent who knew Stratford well. This was mainly because the Stratford branch of that agency was selling houses in the area we wanted. We thought being registered with them would make things easier.

Our children were enjoying volunteering with us once a month at a local Salvation Army care home. We would go as a group from church to worship with the residents on a Sunday afternoon. The elderly residents loved playing with our children, and my daughter (who fancied becoming a doctor like Mummy) got to practice caring for older people. We had no idea our March visit would be the last one for 2020, because we could no longer visit vulnerable care home residents in the pandemic. Care homes were later badly affected by Coronavirus, and many lives were sadly lost. Homes full of elderly people with chronic medical conditions in close proximity were bound to be a favourite place for viruses like Covid-19. At some point, even relatives were not allowed to visit residents, but some people were allowed to speak to each other through the window. Imagine how hard that would have been for 100-year-old Dottie whose only excitement was seeing her great-granddaughter once a week. The heartbreak of the family separations from this pandemic would surely have contributed to some older people giving up on life. Carers also had a hard time worrying about limited availability of Personal Protective Equipment (PPE) initially and risks to their own young families. It really hit home when we heard of young nurses also dying of Covid-19. I think those are the real heroes of 2020.

Although work was busy and emotionally draining with patients' anxieties and reported deaths from Covid-19, I was coping by distracting myself at times on Rightmove, which was now officially an addiction. One Saturday, we went to see three houses near the Stratford school I liked. The estate agents were enthusiastic, but the first two houses just did not seem right for us. We got to the third one, but there was no agent there to meet us. I called the estate agent's office and they sounded surprised we were there. Considering how busy my husband is, and how long we waited to see this particular house, I was not going to take "no" for an answer when they said someone else had already offered to buy the house. We agreed to wait until the agent met us as promised and showed us around. It was perfect for us. Less than five minutes' walk from the school I liked, on a lovely quiet close, with a beautiful, sizable garden and potential for improvements. The few negative points, including dirty looks from one neighbour, were not significant enough to put us off. Our house was already on the market with two viewings booked and we all liked this house, so we put in an offer that week.

How hard could it be? Someone buys my house, I get the cash and buy this "dream house", move house in the summer and the children start their new school in September. Easy, right? No. We got an email to say that schools would be closing on March 27 until further notice. The Prime Minister announced that people should stay at home to reduce the spread of the virus. Restaurants, bars, gyms, leisure centres, theatres and cinemas were told to close. This was the lockdown everyone had been talking about. No more house viewings in lockdown. No school, no shops, no travel, no cinema, no Yoruba class, no restaurants, no visiting people, no gym, no drycleaners, no church, no sports, no salons, no nursery. People were advised to work from home if possible, and only shops selling essential items were to remain open. At least we had sorted the school and house choice before lockdown, I thought. There were rumours about how long schools and businesses could be closed for. September suddenly seemed so far away. Surely, children cannot be off school for 5 months? I had to quickly see my hairdresser to get my hair braided before lockdown, in case this went on as long as some were saying. Even in a pandemic, I wanted to look good!

Sadly, I received news that my uncle in Liverpool had passed away. It did put things into perspective. I needed to be grateful that we still had each other, even in lockdown. Whatever our address, messy hair or not, all that matters is that we are together and well. I prayed for my aunty, who would be alone in lockdown, and phoned to offer her encouragement. I was pleased to hear that she was being well supported by the church in Liverpool. It reminded me of the Bible verse about how God puts the lonely in families.

Loneliness and depression are some of the commonest problems we see in UK General Practice. Mental illness can happen to anyone, but I love how God provides help when we need it, so that things do not have to get too bad. We just have to open up, humble ourselves and receive the support available. God shows us His love through real people he has placed around us. I personally find so much comfort in the words of the Bible, and could not have made it through 2020 without God. Even when doctors have family deaths, we still listen to patients' big and small problems, empathise, and try to help them through our own pain. I was sad to hear that the Prime Minister, Boris Johnson, also tested positive for Coronavirus this month and was unwell with it. I'm sure he too had to keep worrying about the affairs of the nation, even in his illness. Being in a position of leadership and responsibility means that you never get to think only of yourself, but I am so thankful this year for good friends, colleagues, neighbours and family who listened when I needed a listening ear too.

Prince Charles also tested positive for Coronavirus, and the first NHS doctor death from Covid-19 was sadly announced this month too. A temporary NHS Nightingale hospital was set up to help with critical care demand in the pandemic. Retired nurses and doctors around the world heroically offered their services to help fight the pandemic. Mothers' Day was just not the same this year. It is normally a difficult time of year for people who have sadly lost their mums, but it was difficult this year also for many adults who would normally visit their mothers but couldn't do so because of Coronavirus restrictions, and many mothers who had to be at the frontline risking their lives. We were used to just phoning our mothers in Nigeria on Mothers' Day, which is what my husband and I did. Even though distance is sometimes painful, we could still be grateful that they were alive and well. I got a home-cooked meal and a small present because my husband said that was all my children could afford, but that I would get nicer presents when they started working!

One good friend who celebrates her birthday in March and has been like a grandmother to our children could not see us, as usual, this month. She and her family have been friends of our family for years, but we could not meet because of the lockdown. Thankfully, we still had video calls and my children were excited as always to see her. It is also my father's birthday in March, so he gets some extra love too when my mother gets Mothers' Day appreciation. I was pleased this month to hear that one of our lovely patients who tested positive for Coronavirus was back on her feet. She was a devoted carer for her disabled son and spent most of the time worrying about him. Thankfully, she had only mild symptoms and recovered courageously at home in isolation with her son.

There were amazing charities and other organisations providing support for people who needed food and other supplies in isolation, with no close family to help. Even our small village had a phone number for people to call if they needed anything delivered while isolating due to Covid-19. People with Coronavirus symptoms were required to self-isolate for 10 days in 2020 and their contacts were advised to isolate for 14 days. I remember my husband going out to drop off packets of paracetamol for elderly people with arthritis who needed it regularly for pain relief, and many pharmacies were delivering prescription medications for free. This year, more than ever, we saw people obey Jesus' great command to "Love your neighbour as yourself". It was not a year for minding your own business, because we needed to care for each other to get through lockdown together. So many people started praying and looking up to God for the first time. As communities, we realised that we have more resilience and love than we think.

So many things happened for the last time in 2020 this month, and we had no idea it would be the last time. We probably would not have done or said anything differently if we knew, but this just reminds me that it is always good to be good. You never know if your visit to Grandma might be the last one. Studies later showed that the number of people reporting anxiety and depression more than doubled in lockdown. People had been mentioning how they would love to have my motivational self-help book, *Life Without Coffee, Choosing Happiness Over Stress,* as an audiobook. It was mostly people who do not like reading, so I decided to do something about it in lockdown. When else will I have time? I uploaded several Youtube video clips, reading and discussing book excerpts in a *Happiness Over Stress series* to help get people through lockdown in a positive way. So many online Youtube channels got busy in lockdown, and many other services started to go online. People even suggested moving our Wazobia Yoruba language classes online. We decided not to, because there were already many good Yoruba learning channels on Youtube and many of our volunteers were already working so hard in schools and the National Health Service.

I prayed that this Covid-19 pandemic would be over soon, because the thought of long hospital shifts in protective masks and gowns made me worry for my hospital colleagues. Many of them with little children and spouses like mine, worrying about whether they might be exposing their families to infection by staying at work. Some even chose to stay away from their vulnerable family members for months, so that they could continue working. I imagine many junior staff did not have the option of changing work hours or location, even if they wanted to, but there are also people who chose to delay retirement, for example, to work through this pandemic. There were GPs and nurses working in "hot clinics" attending to high-risk Covid-19 patients. All of them deserve our thanks, whether they helped by choice or not. Now that GPs could work from home some days in lockdown, I was grateful for the specialty and work hours I chose. Some of my older retired friends were very disappointed at the fact that they could no longer travel as planned this year. I encouraged them by reminding them that there will hopefully be many more years of fun and travel, if we all stay safe and healthy through this. As a young mum, my main concern was how to keep my children safe and mentally stimulated, while working through lockdown. We had no idea how challenging homeschooling would be over the next few months.

Chapter 4
APRIL
Key Workers

Although most children stayed at home for the UK lockdown, ours were allowed to go to school for childcare because my husband and I are both "key workers". I remember how people waited eagerly for the key workers list to be published on the government website, to find out if they would be eligible for this childcare provision. We realised afresh the value of certain services, without which the nation would come to a standstill. Delivery men, teachers, supermarket workers, nurses, carers, administrators etc. What would we have done without you?! It was good to have the option of lockdown school for our children, but we still had to homeschool because there was mostly no teaching in schools during the first lockdown. It did not take long for me to realise that my children would be getting a rougher deal if we carried on sending them to school daily in lockdown. We were too tired to do the online school work when we got back home each day, they were missing out on time with their parents and they were not making the amazing home memories everyone else in their generation would be talking about in ten years time. This "working mum guilt" really has no end.

There were now over one million confirmed cases of Covid-19 worldwide, which was more than a tenfold increase in less than a month, according to the World Health Organisation. Thankfully, I was able to get everything set up to work from home on days when I was not the GP on call. Most GP consultations were now being done on the phone and only patients that needed face-to-face appointments after telephone triage were being seen in surgery, to reduce risk of Coronavirus spread. Patients were so worried about catching Coronavirus that they would sometimes decline GP face-to-face appointments for fear of going out. Thankfully, most minor ailments could be treated with advice and/or electronic prescriptions sent straight to pharmacies that deliver medications to patients' homes. Even newly qualified GPs like myself had to quickly become very confident in diagnosing conditions based on a good phone history (story of the problem) only. I was reassured by a fact I learned years ago in medical school that 80% of what you need to make a diagnosis comes from the history. Doctors will usually have a good idea of what they think is wrong after speaking with a patient, before they examine patients or order tests to confirm the diagnosis.

Another tip that helped me this year was the fact that not every consultation needed to have a diagnosis. I saw this for myself with many patients booking GP appointments for advice, reassurance or mental health support during the pandemic. This was sometimes even more difficult than treating things like bladder infections, chest infections or diabetes. Establishing a good enough patient-doctor connection to reassure and support people over the phone was sometimes tricky in the time available, but had to be done. There were no visual cues, body language or physical contact, as in face-to-face consultations, which I was used to. The demand for appointments was increasing, and we sometimes had only five minutes per phone call. I occasionally found myself needing a few minutes after some consultations to gather myself, because I was so moved by how hard things were for some people in lockdown. Some patients who tested positive for Coronavirus had months of feeling unwell even after the initial symptoms had cleared. They felt frustrated by the fact that we could not help them with antibiotics for a viral infection. They were not ill enough for hospital admission, but also not well enough to go back to enjoying everyday life. Virtual Covid clinics were eventually set up to monitor patients at home. Uninfected people were allowed to go out for a walk in lockdown, but even that was a source of anxiety for some. Some people's depression, arthritis and obesity got worse with lack of exercise, and they kept requesting higher doses of pain medication. Thankfully, there were some happy patients and simpler requests that made the days easier.

Working from home was a blessing, but it was not easy with two children to homeschool and entertain, especially when everywhere else was closed. I definitely needed God's grace in surplus for this season. Even at the best of times, I am not very keen on looking after children, hence my immense respect for teachers and nursery assistants. I always went back to work from maternity leave as soon as my children needed more mental stimulation, because I would rather pay professionals in the nursery to do that. Days at home with mum always turned to days out for my children. Mine are very energetic and inquisitive, so I would usually have activities planned if we ever had much free time from school/nursery. People often wonder how someone who works as a GP, runs a charity for the education of African children, started a babysitting agency and has two children of her own could be so averse to children's work. I love children really. I just can't wait for them to be good, sensible adults!

I'm thankful that God loves spending time with us, even in times of our own childishness. In fact, Jesus tells us to be child-like in our faith. I tried to keep up my routine of reading my Bible and praying every morning before starting the day, even when we had nowhere to go. I believe my strength comes from having the peace of God in my life. Easter this year was different without the physical church meetings and plays about resurrection Sunday, but we were still grateful to be able to celebrate as a family of four. Queen Elizabeth II gave an inspiring Easter message to the nation, saying: "This year, Easter will be different for many of us but by keeping apart we keep others safe. But Easter isn't cancelled; indeed, we need Easter as much as ever. The discovery of the risen Christ on the first Easter Day gave his followers new hope and fresh purpose, and we can all take heart from this. We know that Coronavirus will not overcome us. As dark as death can be – particularly for those suffering with grief – light and life are greater. May the living flame of the Easter hope be a steady guide as we face the future."

The joy of salvation remained unshakeable for Christians, even in lockdown. Jesus conquered death! I am so grateful that most of my extended family believe in Jesus too, so it was not just about Easter eggs and chocolate for us. I helped my children make Easter hats for the first time this year, thanks to lockdown "free time", but I also made time to talk with them about the real meaning of Easter.

My children loved hearing Bible stories and building their faith in this season, which was a real blessing. As a mother, I was pleased my children were learning to keep body, spirit and soul healthy. I pray they will take these lessons into their adult lives. There are too many people walking around these days with superficial success and smiles, but painful emptiness in their souls.

This month, we got into a morning routine where my children would work through activity books and educational videos while I did my patient consultations from home. We could then have lunch together and enjoy the rest of the day. My children often played nicely together while I cooked, cleaned etc. I was so grateful to have two children in lockdown. I can only imagine how difficult it would have been for me if they did not have each other to play with. Memories of earlier years often crossed my mind. I remembered setting up my Evasitters business while home on maternity leave after my first baby, and writing my book, *Life Without Coffee*, while off on maternity leave with my second baby and toddler. This was nothing like maternity leave. Nothing could have prepared us for this experience of lockdown. There were no playgroups or soft play centres, no cafe meetings with other mums and no visiting friends for a hug.

I remember the stress we all went through when I decided to work full time for some months so that I could complete my GP training in December 2019 instead of the planned May 2020. It was hard on my young family who were used to my working only 3 days a week before that, but we did it by God's grace. Even though I did not know why I felt a strong desire to finish my training earlier, I see now that God really does guide His people. I was so pleased to be able to contribute as a qualified GP in the pandemic, while also being there for my own family. Knowing myself, I know I would not have been very happy to be spending hours at work knowing that my children were missing out on family time this year because of my choices. Their father was working long hours throughout lockdown, but we choose to appreciate the fact that he had work and income, in such times of job insecurity. I really appreciate the many men and women that sacrifice time with family daily to do such busy jobs in health and other sectors.

My children only went to "Coronavirus school" (as my daughter called it) once a week when I was working a full day on call at the surgery. Thankfully, my daughter's school accepted her brother for childcare too, when his nursery closed, even though he was not quite school-aged. God provides our needs, as it says in the popular Bible verse,

Psalm 23:1 “The Lord is my Shepherd, I shall not want”. Their school headteacher and staff were amazingly supportive. There are so many said and unsaid prayers God answered to make 2020 less painful for us as a family, and as a nation too, I believe. There were hard days, but I definitely experienced God's strength and favour through it all.

We were disappointed to get a very low offer from the viewings of our house that happened just before lockdown. I guess with all the uncertainty, no one wanted to buy a house at asking price. I thought it would have been great to have a buyer sorted, so that lawyers working from home could carry on with the house sale and purchase before September. We already found a house we wanted in Stratford, which I was pleased we got to view before lockdown. Our offer was accepted, as well as the earlier offer the seller had for our “dream house”, with the understanding that the house would go to whoever sold theirs and was ready to proceed first. *Fair enough,* I thought initially, but this news of a ridiculously low offer for our house sounded worse when I remembered that there was another offer on our “dream house”. I'm not competitive at all, but come on!!

There were no house viewings allowed in lockdown, so this automatically meant a delay in our moving plans. I felt better knowing that everyone else in the housing market was in the same situation, and realised that we could still be okay for Stratford in September if we managed to find a buyer by June, since house sales were taking around 12 weeks to complete. This is the advantage of planning in advance, I thought. Surely all my busy weeks of viewing schools and houses in Stratford would pay off now. We knew exactly what we wanted and could focus our prayers and efforts on that. Our agent had even sensibly done a video of our house in case any buyers wanted to see it virtually during lockdown. We imagined people would have more time to find houses on Rightmove in lockdown. This would be straightforward, and my children could be Stratford pupils by September, I thought. I can just imagine God listening to my detailed plans then and smiling.

With the rising number of worldwide Covid-19 deaths and social restrictions, I had to cancel our plans for the charity trip to Lagos in May. Even that was another answered prayer. Many organisations were trying to cut losses, but I was not ready to accept any airline vouchers. We got our tickets at a very good price, and I knew we would have to pay at least double if we tried to buy them again later, so I insisted on changing the dates for later in the year when it might be safer to travel. This turned out to be more stressful than I imagined. The online booking agent insisted on offering me vouchers to book flight tickets in future, but I insisted I did not want them. All I wanted was a change of dates. They kept sending me from the booking agent to the airline directly and back. Finally, an angel at the airline changed our flight dates to October half term week, with no additional cost. I knew it was divine intervention when I called back to ask for the tickets by email, and I was told that was not meant to happen! Anyway, flights were sorted - we got our tickets directly from the airline by email, and I could go back to dealing with more pressing issues.

One good thing about the lockdown was that we had time for more video calls with our family members in Nigeria. I was very sad to hear that one of our close family friends passed away. He was a pastor at my home church and had been struggling with his health for a while. I saw him at my sister's wedding in Nigeria in December, and had even partnered with his charity to help some orphaned children in Kaduna. I was so heartbroken by this news, it took a lot for me to work that week. I am not one who is quick to take time off work for personal issues, because I genuinely look forward to doing my job, but I considered it that week. I would have taken time off work if I really felt too low to help anyone, but I felt God comforting me from the inside, even when tears came to my eyes while talking to bereaved or struggling patients that week. Thankfully, my work colleagues were also very supportive during this difficult time. I imagine the challenges of the pandemic this year facilitated our quick bonding into what felt like my work family. I have learned from the Bible and from life experience that people being sick or dying does not mean that God does not care. God is good all the time, and His ways are higher than ours. We may not find all the answers to our questions on this side of eternity, but we can be sure of God's love in every situation.

It was actually nice to have a break from after-school clubs, and just relax at home together after homeschooling. Between music lessons, gymnastics, swimming and dance classes, children these days need their own personal assistants. Lockdown helped us to reassess what activities were really worth continuing, especially because these things cost money as well. Payment for everything else was cancelled, but we kept paying a token to keep our swimming class slots. I finally managed to get my two children the same swimming class time slot last month, and I was not about to lose it. We used to have the boy's lesson at 4pm and the girl's at 4.30pm, so I had to stick around the humid leisure centre for over an hour. Now I could have them both in the new pool for swimming classes in two stages at 4pm and be home before 5pm. That's what I call time management. Even though there is only a two-year gap between my children, it was always difficult to get similar class times for activities they wanted to do. Swimming with them at the hotel pool was fun for a few weeks, but I had to let them go back to proper swimming lessons last month when I realised the girl was already swimming better than me!

My children decided that we needed a "No phones day" one weekend, and we all agreed. Children these days can be deprived of eye contact when we spend so much time on our phones and computers. This is something we are consciously trying to reduce as adults in our home, but it is still a challenge with so many emails and notifications. My daughter can't wait to be old enough to have a phone, and I worry that she might totally ignore me when she does, if I do not learn to control my phone habits around them now. I tried to be good and send all my messages before they woke up, so there was no phone for me all day that day. I guess I could have used my Bible app and camera as excuses to use my phone during the day, but I am pleased to say that I didn't. Their father was the most tempted to cheat, but we both could not wait for the children to go to bed that night, so we could go back to our nice toys.

The slower pace of lockdown allowed me to watch some popular movies with my children in the afternoons. I remember days before lockdown when I felt life was too busy, and I looked forward to weekends to be able to show them a movie I really liked as a child. We went all out this time, and even subscribed to Disney plus. We also watched *The Greatest Showman* so many times, because it became a favourite musical in our house. I'm sure the songs from that movie will always remind us of 2020. To be more productive whilst watching so many movies, I decided to finish the scarf I started knitting for my husband 4 years ago! A few years ago, I lost a handmade scarf he really loved and promised to replace it, but life had become too busy for knitting. It was nice to be able to finally complete his black scarf in lockdown, and even show my daughter how to knit. I remember there was a clock in our lounge during lockdown that said "Enjoy the little moments in life because one day you will look back and realise they were the big ones". I am truly grateful for those moments now.

I secretly even enjoyed having no visitors or playdates in lockdown. We had time to catch up on many things. Our neighbours told us how people in the village were spending more time on their allotments, and looking after their mental health that way. The allotments became so popular, they even had a waiting list. Some people had the allotments as a good way to spend time safely outdoors in lockdown, while others enjoyed the harvest during food shortages. Gardening was a popular hobby for my patients in lockdown, especially with the surprisingly good weather for this time of year. The sunshine reminded me so much that God cares. We saw many "NHS rainbows" put up by children in house windows when we went for walks. The rainbows were a sign of hope in tough times, but they often reminded me of God's rainbow promise in the Bible, that He would never again flood the earth like in the time of Noah. To be honest, we are not more righteous than the people of those days. I am grateful for God's mercy that we were not all consumed by this pandemic. Besides, the sacrifice of Jesus means that we have hope for eternal life in heaven even when our lives here on earth come to an end.

My children were still able to see some friends on Zoom and during our local walks, but my diary was not full of meetings anymore. Zoom became a big thing with church and work meetings happening virtually. I am sure many people were secretly glad to have some meetings cancelled, especially those meetings you could have just sent an email about. It took some time for people to get comfortable with the Zoom platform, but it became normal after a few weeks. Even my patients were happy to have video consultations now. We started enjoying online church meetings on Sundays, but I personally missed the physical corporate worship meetings. People also started having Zoom parties for birthdays, and people who organise meetings for things you could just say in an email soon started doing that with Zoom!

I started doing Youtube workouts at home with the children for exercise, as I was not too keen on walking in the beautiful woods near us. Crazy, I know, but it is just not my thing. The thought of insect bites, leaves touching me or getting lost in the woods with no phone signal was not helping either. Our children often played in the garden, and I sometimes walked with them to the shops. Some of the lyrics to the songs on those workout videos were not good when repeated by children, so I found some Christian zumba videos. We later discovered Leslie Sansone's *Walk at Home* videos that I still love to do with my daughter. She continued having violin lessons on Zoom but motivation was declining, so we signed her up for a virtual orchestra, which her tutor was kindly supportive of. There were a few challenging pieces for a five-year-old, but she stuck with it while counting down to her sixth birthday in May.

As much as I enjoy writing, blogging on my daughter's school website to keep teachers updated about our home-schooling was not my favourite thing to do. I was the annoying parent who just sent an email once in a while to let them know the children were still learning. I think they assumed it was because of my busy GP job. My addiction to Rightmove was still there. I knew about almost every new house that came up for sale in Stratford. It was fun looking at the floor plans, gardens etc, and seeing if there was anything else we might like. It was now four whole weeks of no house viewings, and we were all just waiting to see how things would progress with the pandemic. I must have mistakenly prayed for patience last year, because it seems that is what God was trying to teach me this year.

Psalm 27.14
Wait patiently for the Lord. Be brave and courageous.
Yes, wait patiently for the Lord.

Chapter 5
MAY
Quarantine birthdays

After a few weeks indoors, it was announced that there would be phased easing of the lockdown as daily numbers of recorded Covid-19 deaths started coming down and the UK had gone "past the peak", but we still needed to "stay alert". There was news of the start of human trials of a Coronavirus vaccine, which we hoped would do well. The government was also working on providing access to more Coronavirus testing and a contact tracing app. Social media was full of opinions from people who felt they could do a better job than the Prime Minister. That was definitely one job I did not want this year. So many major decisions, with so many factors to consider. Even though we needed tight restrictions to control the Coronavirus pandemic, there were also effects on education, mental health, economy and so on to consider. It was a balancing act; a bit like how we weigh risk versus benefit in medicine when we give toxic medications to treat disease. Making such decisions with one patient is difficult enough with many aspects of their one life to consider. I imagined it would be so much harder making such big decisions for a nation full of people from different backgrounds with differing priorities. I'm sure it would have been easier just to let everyone do whatever they thought was right, and see what or who was left after the pandemic!

Thankfully, our government did not leave us to our own devices and most people seemed to be following government guidance. It was announced this month that people would be allowed to go for exercise more than once a day and sunbathe in parks. Thank God for lovely weather during lockdown. I am sure depression and anxiety rates would have more than tripled if families were stuck indoors in the cold, dark months. We were warned to keep two metres away from each other and wear face coverings in enclosed places. There was a rise in judgemental social media posts about people not doing the right thing. It was nothing to do with education or social class, because there were a few people secretly breaking rules everywhere. I found it funny that many people also felt the need to add, "socially-distanced, of course" when describing the social activities they wanted to share online this month, so that they would not be labelled irresponsible, yet they felt comfortable sharing drunkenness stories and inappropriate photos without any explanation.

I was happy at the thought of non-essential shops possibly reopening soon, as Covid-19 statistics improved. Even a trip to the supermarket used to be good enough for us as something fun to do together. That was no longer fun, because you now had to wear face-coverings, wait in queues to be let in without overcrowding the store, try not to touch anything you won't buy and ignore the palpable Coronavirus fear in an enclosed space, where you dare not cough! I had my children with me almost all the time in lockdown, so they had to go with me if I ever needed to go into shops, especially now that we could not get any slots for online food shop deliveries.

"I can't believe someone would bring their children here!" a lady in the shop muttered.

"Excuse me. Are children not allowed in Tesco now?" I said.

"Oh, they are. It's okay." She replied, sheepishly.

This was the kind of attitude some people were giving others, without knowing people's personal circumstances. While most neighbourhoods and communities pulled together to support each other during restrictions, some people had made themselves in charge of making others feel bad for the way they did things in lockdown. I love how "polite" British people often get shocked when you confront their murmurings. This lady had no idea who she was talking about, and somehow thought that she could possibly care about the health of my own children more than I do. I already had enough on my mind with all the news about black men and women being more likely to die a Coronavirus-related death than white people. I was not just black, but also a health worker, married to another black health worker, trying to keep safe in a pandemic with small children. The minimal Personal Protective Equipment we were getting this month as NHS workers was not exactly inspiring confidence in our chances of making it. I did not think it was too much to ask for us to have fresh food to eat while working through the pandemic. Maybe I was just a bit grumpy today. Help me, God!

Supermarkets introduced the early "NHS staff shopping hour", but there were times my family had to eat some very unusual meals for lack of our usual ingredients on the shop shelves. At least, we had food! The thought of people having to do food rationing during wartime years ago made me grateful that things were not that bad. It is always easier to be grateful when you realise things really could be worse. I was aware of families who were struggling financially in lockdown, even with the government furlough scheme, where 80% of wages was paid to people who could not work due to the pandemic restrictions. Some families had to depend on free school meals, which were thankfully continued in lockdown. There was a period of shortages of things like toilet roll, flour and tinned tomatoes. Some people had overstocked their homes for lockdown and stores ran out. Supermarkets had to put a limit on the maximum number of certain items we could buy, to allow for others to get some. It is amazing how selfish we can become as humans when we panic. Thankfully, most people calmed down and continued to care for the wider community again. People tried to shop reasonably, and even donated to food banks in this season.

Demand for food banks and free school meals increased with loss of jobs in the pandemic. Some families who were barely getting by sadly had to make even more cuts to survive. There was concern for the effects of lockdown and school closures on the education of disadvantaged children, who had no access to personal laptops or internet for learning at home. When poor families were struggling to feed growing children stuck at home all day, it was hard to imagine them forking out money for computers for school work. Sadly some of those parents did not even consider education a priority, and would even tell doctors that cigarettes were more important for their sanity. We had many more requests for doctors' notes to support benefits (social welfare) applications. This pandemic caused serious and unexpected hardship for some hard-working people. If that was you, I would just like to encourage you here to please stay hopeful, keep doing your best with what you have and things will get better.

Many of us who normally used supermarket home delivery slots for convenience had to give them up, because there were shielding, disabled, isolating and elderly people who really needed them. Because my husband was also on the list of "vulnerable people", he only went to and from work, so I went everywhere else for us. I was eventually able to go to the supermarket on my own at weekends when things settled down a bit for us, and we later discovered "click and collect" supermarket slots which used to be all gone by the morning if you did not wait up till midnight to get one in lockdown. Shopping was no longer fun with social distancing. We all had to get used to shopping online. Amazon Prime next-day deliveries became very popular.

At least, people born in and after May had time to get used to the fact that there would be no birthday parties this summer. My daughter and I celebrate our birthdays a week apart in May. I had planned a *Claire's Accessories* make up party for my daughter, but had to cancel it. She decided she wanted a Jasmine dress for her birthday. Like many mums, I went all out and did a themed lockdown family-of-four birthday celebration. The supermarket had everything I needed, and we could still order personalised cakes online. Even her Afro got special attention with hair straighteners which she wanted us to use on her birthday. My little daughter looked 16 instead of six, with her beautiful hair and Jasmine outfit. Some of her little friends from school stopped by on their walks to say 'Happy birthday', which was very sweet and made me think how much we would miss this village when we eventually moved. I was feeling very peaceful about the house sale situation this month and decided to trust God's timing for it. There were no further house viewings as lockdown continued, and our estate agent reported that there was no further interest registered online either. At least, we had birthday cakes to cheer us up!

My daughter really enjoyed her birthday and spent hours playing with her kids' makeup, which surprisingly was delivered on her actual birthday despite my late order. Little timings like this often remind us that God cares. I was struggling to get a refund for the makeup party deposit, so I decided to let my daughter buy some children's makeup online the week before. It is amazing how much six-year-old girls like makeup these days. I didn't even know what makeup was at that age! I guess today's girls want to be like their makeup-wearing mums. My mother never really wore makeup, and my Dad did not like it, so it was not a thing in our house. My daughter was allowed to play with her own makeup at home, but it was not to be worn outdoors. She also had to stay away from mum's real makeup. She is a good girl and often does as she is told. It is just funny to watch how she can spend a long time doing her makeup, and then gladly wipe it off before we go out. I guess time is not that precious when you are six!

Many little things happened in lockdown which reminded me of God's love for us in this difficult time. My daughter mentioned that she wanted to be on television, so I let her upload a video of her violin playing on Youtube. She was so pleased to see herself on our big TV screen playing *Twinkle Twinkle Little Star*, but God had a better gift. Her virtual orchestra performance of the *Good Morning Britain* theme song was aired on live television that week, and she even got a mention as the youngest member! Looking back now, I realise that we both had special birthdays, even in lockdown. When we focus on what we have instead of what we do not, we see that God is so good to us. He is not a genie, and He does not have to do anything for us. My life and salvation is more than enough already, yet He cares so much, even about the little things we desire.

Many big parties and events were cancelled this year. I could honestly feel the pain for people who planned weddings, milestone birthday parties, entertainment events and examinations. It takes so much to organise these things, and I am sure the effort needed to undo all the plans was not insignificant. My close May-born friends decided with me to have a restaurant dinner later in the year to celebrate, when possible. My husband did very well by getting me a beautiful dress for my birthday. I put it on, with matching makeup, to enjoy dinner at home celebrating with my three favourite people. For me, this was probably better than having a big party this year. Some lovely friends also dropped off birthday cards/ presents for my daughter and I, as well as kind wishes on social media. Even though there was much we could not do for or with each other in 2020, the little acts of love meant much more in times like these.

I was glad to have Spotify on my phone to play encouraging Christian music every day, reminding me of God's steadfast love and goodness. I was particularly encouraged by the song, *Waymaker* by Sinach. It was even better when a version was released by Michael W. Smith, adding that God is working even when we don't see it. It can be hard to see God at work when most of what we hear is bad news and complaining on TV, but I was so grateful for our good health. I remember a tough week last year when my husband was hospitalised with a terrible chest infection before Covid-19 officially hit the UK. He was isolated on the respiratory ward, and I even had to wear Personal Protective Equipment to visit him without the children because doctors were not sure of the cause. My husband took days to respond to even the strongest antibiotics intravenously, and we had the whole church praying for him. Our miracle-working God cleared my husband's lungs and healed him, without the need for intensive care or chest drains. Knowing my husband's medical history, I knew it was indeed a miracle. Would we have doubted God's love if he ended up in ITU or dead? No! God's love endures forever. Sometimes we do not understand why bad things happen, but we can surely trust that God loves us and works all things together for the good of those who love him, as the Bible says in Romans 8.28. I can definitely say that this experience last year made us more thankful for our lives and health in 2020. God's mercy is much more than we deserve. We were also able to be more empathetic and helpful when dealing with patients and families in similar situations as healthcare professionals.

There was not much going on in terms of my charity work for Forte because schools and universities were closed, here and abroad. We asked new applicants in Nigeria to reapply for grants after resumption, if still needed. We were also limited in terms of fundraising activities, because of the social restrictions. Children from the Yoruba language school were missing each other, but we had a phone Whatsapp group to keep in touch with families and volunteers. I informed them that we might be able to do the Forte Charity annual fundraising *Walk to School* in the summer, if government guidance allowed. I quite enjoyed a restful season this month, and chose not to do any extra sessions outside of my main GP job. I was blessed to be able to do that, because we intentionally kept our basic family expenses low so that we would not be desperate for extra income in times like these. God's provision in this season even meant that we were able to give and save more, because of less expenses from reduced childcare costs and not going out during lockdown.

If cameras really did steal a piece of our soul, we would all have been soulless after lockdown. There were so many videos and photos being shared on social media, because we had more free time, and spent more time with our beautiful children. I was enjoying making my *Happiness Over Stress* video clips, with my husband's help, and it was good to hear feedback about how the content was helping people reflect on their lifestyles and choices during lockdown. We also did some videos as part of a church series on the book of Mark, and I enjoyed watching videos from others sharing what they felt God had been saying to them from the Bible this year too. Having church online was still taking some getting used to, but the peaceful presence of God was evident in our homes. It made me think of the days when the early disciples met in each other's homes for fellowship. Even though no one was actually coming into our house, I still felt the need to always keep it tidy and presentable. Having a tidy home definitely helped to maintain my sanity while spending so much time indoors.

This month, I finally had a chance to catch up with one of my best friends from secondary school who still lived in Nigeria. I told her about our postponed plans to visit Lagos, and she planned to join us for the seminars whenever we came. It was good to hear her story also about how God changed her life after secondary school. She was now a born again Christian with a family of her own. Her passion was for empowering women in the workplace by finding their purpose in God. I was privileged to edit her book, which was about letting your God-given purpose lead you to a more fulfilling career. It is true about never having to work a day in your life if you do what you love, but it is even better to be serving the world around you through what you do. Sometimes we get caught up in a dark place because we look only at ourselves and what we can gain. When we focus on God and others, there is always more to be joyful and thankful for.

We had a half-term break from homeschooling, and it was great. I had also finished my work audit, which I was so pleased to have on my eportfolio when the doctors' regulatory body decided GPs should have appraisals later this year. I felt so blessed to be able to work from home and still be contributing as a healthcare worker, also releasing my husband to be more available at the front line, but I sometimes felt jealous of those who were not working, especially when they kept calling doctors for no good reason - taking up appointments that others might have needed. There were even a few patients who were meant to be working, but tried to find every excuse to get a doctor's note to stay home with their families in lockdown sunshine. The reality was that my job was a real blessing in lockdown. People like me would not just go crazy with prolonged idleness, I might have murdered Coronavirus myself!

I was also thankful that all the renovations we planned for our house were done before lockdown, so we enjoyed being home. Many people got a lot of DIY renovations done in lockdown and some put their houses on the market after that. I had several patients calling up with aches and sprains sustained while fixing things around their houses. For us, it was good to be able to just enjoy being in the house. I loved watching the children playing in the garden, on the trampoline and with the chickens. We had dinner together at the dining table and read at bedtime with the children as usual, but it was nice not to have to rush through those special moments. There were no more meetings, restaurants or events to rush to after work. When we drove to work, the roads were so quiet. Supermarket car parks had so many parking spaces to choose from. Bus stations and train stations were almost empty. City centre was terribly quiet. Even airports were deserted in lockdown. Pubs were all closed, and we learned to enjoy "home sweet home".

The slow pace of lockdown really made me think that we could do with a less busy diary as a family. There were more houses going on Rightmove, probably also because people were realising the importance of home office spaces and gardens. With so many large organisations restructuring to allow their staff to work from home, it looked like we might not need to have so many cars on the roads after lockdown. I just hoped that someone would be dreaming of my house as much as I was dreaming of the house we liked in Stratford-upon-Avon.

1 Peter 5:6-7
So humble yourselves under the mighty power of God, and at the right time he will lift you up in honour. Give all your worries and cares to God, for He cares about you.

Chapter 6
JUNE
Summer days

As lockdown measures were slowly eased, children in Reception, Year 1 and Year 6 were allowed to return to school before the end of the academic year. Despite all the complaints about the challenges of homeschooling, some parents preferred to keep their children with them at home, because of ongoing worries about Coronavirus infections. We were having daily Prime Minister updates, which I had stopped watching by now, because there was always a summary of the key points in the news. Friends kept asking if I was going to let my children go to school, but people like us did not have the option of keeping them completely away. Some key workers had their children in schools everyday, mixing with other "high risk" families throughout lockdown because they had to go into work to keep the country going. Even though we were told that Covid-19 symptoms were usually mild in children, I did not find it funny when someone joked that they would wait to see what happened to the first set of children to go back before sending theirs in.

Thankfully, most children remained well and I did not encounter any serious child cases of Coronavirus among my patients. Coronavirus testing was not widely available at this point, so everyone just isolated if they developed mild symptoms. The main symptoms were a new dry, continuous cough and fever, but an interesting other symptom was added to the list later. A loss or change in sense of smell or taste. After a few weeks in school, it seemed some people saw that our children were still alive and started fighting for theirs to come back to school when they also struggled to manage their behaviour at home. Unfortunately, not everyone who wanted a place could get one, because of social distancing and number limitations to maintain bubbles. Our little village school did really well in supporting parents and providing childcare earlier in lockdown. They had to close at some point because it was just us and another family who needed childcare, so we were asked to go to the school in the next village for a few weeks. I am still so proud of my children's resilience through all this. They made friends easily and got so many compliments from the teachers there, who were particularly impressed with my daughter's level of reading for her age. The boy was just a cute charmer everywhere. At only three, he could make a menopausal woman feel 16 with the thoughtful compliments he gives.

My son's nursery had closed until this month, and thankfully did not charge us for last month. I could hear the pain in people's voices when they spoke about how much other nurseries and private schools were charging them while their children stayed at home. We were pleased to have our local nursery reopen this month, so my son could see some of his friends for his June birthday. I often call him "our referendum baby" because he was born on June 23 when the UK voted for Brexit in 2016. He does not mind the referendum part, but now tells me at almost four that he is not a baby! I remember my husband keenly stopping at the village hall for me to vote, as we drove home from hospital with our new baby that day. I'm sure the people who fought for women's rights to vote did not expect that some of us would be exercising that right immediately after giving birth to an eight-pound baby.

I had some patients tell me how their local schools were being very good and taking in children that did not meet the general criteria for returning to school this term because their families were struggling at home. It was sometimes a child with behavioural problems, or due to parental mental health problems. I was pleased to see that the welfare of children and families remained a priority for schools and the government. As much as we want children to do well and not miss out on their education, we have to also remember their need for emotional health, without which children cannot reach their full potential in school. Several children had lost grandparents and other loved ones in the pandemic, so it was important for us to ensure they were coping well mentally first before trying to feed their brains with knowledge. Children often pick up on their parents' subconscious cues, so it seemed that parents who were calmer and in control seemed to have less anxious children.

I was so pleased to hear on the news that retail parks and non-essential shops were definitely re-opening this month. I gladly shopped online in lockdown, but have always preferred being able to see what I was buying. I think my husband was more concerned about our bank account when he heard this news. Our nearest retail park closed at 8pm, so I imagined I could get some alone time in the shops if I went immediately after my husband came home from work one evening. Retail therapy was back on. I could also get some books with the children from charity shops while the libraries were closed. They would often read through all their new books within a few days, so we would go once or twice a month to donate books and buy more. When the clothes stores finally reopened, my child-free retail therapy shopping trip was not as good as I imagined it. It felt more like I was trying to rob the stores, with my face mask and their new Covid-19 no-trying-on policy. I had now been converted to a proper online shopper, which was actually more dangerous for our bank account, at all hours of the night.

I planned a trip to Wales for my son's birthday this year so he could see dinosaur caves, but the venue was still closed due to the pandemic. Thankfully, zoos and safari parks reopened this month. I remember staying up late till past midnight on the day our closest safari park was to reopen, so that I could get family tickets for the weekend of my son's birthday. The tickets were half price because only the safari part would open initially, so visitors would have to stay in their cars for the drive-through experience. My children had recently read about safari parks, and I thought it would be great to take them. Saturday was always a popular choice for family activities, and there were other determined mothers like me out there, so unsurprisingly, the website was jammed all night. My husband thought I was crazy for being so keen on these tickets, but God did not - because He let me get some the next day.

The excitement on my children's faces when I told them about the safari park tickets was priceless. They had missed going out like this. My daughter even told me that the first place she would want to fly to after the pandemic would be America. She really enjoyed our last visit to Florida and kept talking about wanting to live there. Sadly, there had been lots of worrying news from America with the cruel death of a black man called George Floyd at the hands of a white police officer, which raised serious concerns and discussion about institutional and widespread racism. There was heavy campaigning by the *Black Lives Matter* movement in the media. Even people who "forgot" they were black were suddenly reminded of their skin colour and forced to speak out. We all had to pay more attention to the issues being raised, especially as parents raising black children in the western world. Most of our friends and neighbours are white, so it was heartwarming to get encouraging and supportive messages from those who were outraged by this injustice.

I remember one black patient of mine who really struggled in this season because she was married to a white man, and was beginning to see a deeper meaning to certain aspects of their relationship and interactions with his family. People were forced to really think about their own attitudes to race and stereotypes. I had to do some soul-searching myself, because as a confident Nigerian-British doctor, I did not fully understand the plight of those who had grown up black in a mostly white society, experiencing discrimination and disadvantage even before they could speak up for themselves. Some useful documentaries came up on Netflix, and I was glad we had time to discuss some of the issues with our own children at their level. Their school was also doing a good job speaking to all the children about this. I strongly felt that this was an issue worth tackling now, no matter how painful to discuss. It is not okay just to be "nice to black people". As someone said - people can be nice to their dogs too. We need to treat all humans with respect. Black lives do matter.

I found comfort, as always, in God. Seeing a video of such an inhumane killing of someone who looks like you definitely shakes you inside, but Jesus helps us to love and forgive. I added my voice and spoke out against the injustice on social media, at work and wherever I could, because "the only thing necessary for the triumph of evil is for good men to do nothing". It was reassuring to be surrounded by so many enlightened and godly people. There was no argument. Racism was not to be tolerated wherever I questioned it. One of my Nigerian friends was working as a doctor at a new practice and told me how a female patient called back asking to speak to an "English doctor" after a phone consultation with my Nigerian friend. I was so annoyed to hear this, especially because I know he is a good doctor. She did not report any concerns about the advice the Nigerian doctor gave her, but she just wanted advice from an English doctor. I was pleased to hear that my friend reported the matter and got an apology, because the receptionist who rebooked the appointment and the "English doctor" who spoke to the patient again should not have encouraged this. Subtle things like this erode confidence, respect and opportunities for people from minority ethnic groups, and should not be tolerated. I suspect the receptionists at my own surgery would have told her to try Buckingham Palace!

Doctors find it helpful when GP receptionists make a note of the reason for a phone call when booking GP appointments. As most of our consultations were by phone these days, I could go more straight to the point if the booking had the main complaint written next to the patient's name and phone number on the appointments page. The actual complaint was sometimes very different from what the patient told the receptionist but thankfully, not too often. Some patients would just tell the receptionist that their problem was "private", which often caught my curiosity. One gentleman was open enough to tell the receptionist it was about his erectile dysfunction. I laughed out loud alone in my office when I saw "*reptile* dysfunction" written next to his name. Typing errors we all make in medical note-taking can make for great comedy, but this gentleman did not find it funny when I asked about his ethnicity while discussing his hypertension. These days, you cannot assume that a man called David Smith is white, or that a woman called Sophie Adebayo is black. Also in England, even children of first-generation immigrants like myself sound "proper British", especially on the phone. I actually had to ask, because it was important information for his treatment. The clinical guidelines clearly advise doctors, based on evidence, to use different antihypertensives for people aged 55 years or over, and people of black African or African-Caribbean family origin (of any age). Before the Coronavirus pandemic, I could just make my decision while sitting in front of the patient, but this was now another interesting question to ask over the phone. With all the campaigns against racism this year, I always had to ask this carefully. I just hope that calling people black and white will still be politically correct by the time you read this. Apologies in advance, if not. I still get called a "nice coloured doctor" by well-meaning elderly white patients, who have no idea which terms are acceptable these days.

Places of worship and car showrooms also reopened this month. I say this in one sentence, not because there is any correlation, but now that I think about it, a funny quote comes to my mind - "Just like sitting in a garage does not make you a car, going to church does not make you a

Christian". And it is true. Christians are people who believe in Jesus Christ, God's only son as their saviour, and choose to follow His Holy Spirit's leading in every area of their lives. Our small group of Christians normally rents space on a Sunday morning at a music school for corporate worship. We had to continue with online church services this month in spite of the relaxed rules because we do not own a "place of worship". This challenged me to be more committed to praying for a church building of our own. Our church also worked with other churches for the *Open Heaven Coventry* prayer walks to pray for families on every single street of the city this month. I was very proud of how our church had stepped up to the challenge, also producing great quality online material for Sunday mornings that we could share with the world. The church is indeed not about the building, but people whose hearts are devoted to Jesus and one another in love. As the rules allowed socially-distanced meetings outdoors, we met up with other families in parks to catch up. We were to stay two metres away from people outside our households, but it was usually hard to enforce this among the younger children. Seeing each other in the sunshine was definitely better than Zoom meetings.

One of the things I will miss most about our little village is the community spirit. Everyone looks out for each other here. I hope all Warwickshire villages and towns are like this, and that we will have friendly neighbours in Stratford when we eventually move. We still had no house viewings since lockdown, but the pandemic and other issues were higher up on our minds at this point. It was heartwarming to see many of our neighbours last month for VE day celebrations on the street. Everyone knew we wanted to move, with the horrible 'For Sale' sign in front of our house. I really hated it. I told our closest neighbours we were planning to put the house on the market, but I hoped that it would be a quick sale with no need for the signboard. The 'For Sale' sign was put up after a few weeks to help marketing. Our neighbours kept telling me how they did not want us to move, because they would miss us. I would genuinely miss them too, but I really felt like it was time for a change, so "please stop counteracting my prayers", I told them - nicely, of course. I did not want the "good" we had here to become the enemy of "best" we could have, as some say. This was a good time to start thinking about secondary schools and the bigger picture. We loved this house and village, but we were also trying to do what we felt was best for our family long term, even if it was not easy. We would still be in Warwickshire and definitely planned to keep in touch with the amazing friends we had made over the years.

We celebrated my son's birthday with pizza and cake at home on June 23, and heard the Prime Minister's final daily Coronavirus press conference. My boy was so kind and shared his presents with his big sister to avoid any repercussions later, as only younger siblings know about. Some of his friends from nursery school stopped by with presents, and we gave them some cake too. I was not just being generous, I was really trying to avoid having more cake in the house after eating so much cake from our two birthdays last month. My children looked forward to seeing animals at the safari park at the weekend, but there were now photos on the news showing people ignoring social distancing rules and crowding beaches in the hot weather. I hoped people would be more sensible, so we would not need tougher restrictions again. I was enjoying the freedom to be able to go to shops and do some house viewings in Stratford while waiting for a buyer. I even sorted out a solicitor for the conveyancing, so that there would be no delay on my part once we got a good offer - that was faith in action.

My parents normally visit us for a few weeks from Nigeria in the summer, but thankfully they had planned a Christmas visit to the UK this year. There was no way they would have been able to fly here in the current state of things. We also heard on the news that travellers were now being required to quarantine for 14 days upon arrival into the UK. One of the houses we viewed in Stratford reminded me so much of the kind of houses we have in Nigeria. It was fenced and tastefully designed, but it was not close to the school I really liked. My daughter loved it because it had a pink playhouse in the garden, but my husband was not keen because he wanted a project he could improve on. I did some online research and found out that the school near the fenced house was ranked higher than the school I wanted, but no one was showing parents around schools anymore. I would normally never send my children to a school I had not physically visited but I liked this fenced house so much, I was willing to make an exception. I kept the brochure for the fenced house by my bedside and prayed that God would send a buyer for ours soon so we could get this house. This was plan B after I found out that our Stratford "dream house" had sold. Maybe this was a better house and school than what we originally wanted, and maybe God did not let us sell sooner, so we could find this one. All sorts of thoughts go through an impatient woman's mind.

Work was going well this month. I had very good feedback from our senior GP partner at my six-month work review. Apparently, not many patients were missing appointments with me, and many were coming back to see me again. I never knew these things could be measured, and I was not sure if patients coming back to see me was definitely a good thing. I imagined that some patients would come back because a GP was saying what they wanted to hear, while others came back because they would have come back to any other GP. Anyway, I chose to take the compliment about being liked as a GP and keep working hard. I was going into the surgery three days a week now that school and nursery were open. Working from home was easier on the other two days, because the children were not home. I later decided to go in every day when both of them started school in September, because I did not have to be at home anymore, and it was easier to bring in patients for face-to-face appointments sooner this way.

I was so grateful that car showrooms had opened again, when my husband came home one day to tell me that he had a car crash and his car was irreparable! Thankfully, no one was hurt, and the car was only an insurance write-off because of the nature of the damage and the age of the car. I had suggested getting a new car for him months ago, but he insisted there was no need. While he lamented about having to find a new car to buy, I was secretly happy we were finally getting rid of that old car of his. He pointed out that he might have crashed a new car if he listened and got a new car when I wanted, but I told him, he might have never had a crash if he had got the new car, because this might have been the only way to get him to buy another car. Trust me to always see the bright side.

I took a break from my Rightmove addiction and moved on to Autotrader to help him find a decent second-hand car, since we had decided against brand new cars for now. We eventually found a Peugeot he liked in Bradford, where my aunt lived. We got a rental car so we could visit my aunt - on the doorstep, due to Covid-19 rules - then drive over to get the new car, if we liked it. Thankfully, it was better than we thought, so we bought it and returned the rental car there. God always provides for His people. The icing on the cake for me was that my husband finally agreed to use the personalised car registration plate I got him for our wedding anniversary last year, so we now had matching number plates like teenagers in love.

As our tenth wedding anniversary was less than four weeks away, I also convinced my husband to come with me to the jewellers to check ring sizes. I had been hinting for months about this lovely sapphire ring I wanted. Sometimes, when you have been married this long, you can't trust that hinting alone will work, so I showed him the exact ring I liked. No need for subtlety in marriage, I think. I knew it would be only me who would have a bad day if he got it wrong, so I sacrificed my female dignity and said exactly what I wanted for once. I think he appreciated that. This mind-reading skill we think men have is a serious misconception.

I also used the opportunity to confirm his ring size for an heirloom signet ring I had been eyeing for his birthday next month. We bought the cheapest gold wedding rings when we got married, but I have to say that the rings were truly blessed. I am thankful that our marriage has remained happy in spite of the ups and downs of life and lockdown. I have seen friends' and patients' marriages break up this year, and it is truly heartbreaking news, especially where children are involved. I guess some marriages already had serious cracks that were exposed by life in lockdown. Many divorced people talk about how happy they are on their own, but as doctors, we get the rare privilege of hearing what they really think on the lonely, tough days, or at the end of their lives. Let's stop pretending that divorce is not painful, and be there for those who need our support. We have had to grow and compromise by God's grace to accommodate each other in marriage, but I believe having Jesus as leader of our lives and home is the main reason why we are still enjoying marriage, and for this I give double thanks and pray for the same joy for others.

I heard a comedian joke about how women should not get married before the age of 27 because that is when their brains fully develop. I got married at the age of 26, while my "underdeveloped" brain (according to this) was still learning to be a doctor. Others my age had already been practising medicine for years and giving advice to married people. Marriage is such a complex subject and there is no simple formula for a happy marriage, but I know for sure that a successful marriage has nothing to do with intelligence. In fact, I think intelligent women struggle more with the concept of being united in marriage with a mere man! If marriage was better with the stage of brain development at entry, surely people who got married in their 30s or 40s would have better marriages; and those in their 2nd or 3rd marriages would always be much happier. Not true! Have you ever seen an old couple fight? It is not pretty. They can be meaner than young couples, with painful words and proper grudges. I think marriages work better when we follow the manufacturer's manual. Surely, God who invented marriage must know the best way to make it work, and the Bible has so much unpopular wisdom about this. Marriage is a matter of faith - faith that your spouse will always stand by you, that your in-laws do not secretly hate you, and that you will not actually kill your spouse on the days you feel you could! Thank God for His grace on the difficult days.

I Corinthians 13: 4 - 8

Love is patient, love is kind. It does not envy, it does not boast, it is not proud. It does not dishonour others, it is not self-seeking, it is not easily angered, it keeps no record of wrongs. Love does not delight in evil but rejoices with the truth. It always protects, always trusts, always hopes, always perseveres. Love never fails.

Chapter 7
JULY
Ten years already

We were excited to have made it into the second half of this year in good health. This is still the season for celebrations in my family, because July is the month of my husband's birthday and our wedding anniversary. Our daughter's hands were sore from excessive hand washing, and hand sanitizer gels were selling for ridiculous prices, but we had to keep doing our best to reduce the spread of Coronavirus and get back to some kind of normal as a country soon. Hotels were allowed to re-open, so we planned a night away for our anniversary weekend. As we could not have babysitters in the pandemic, we had to take our children with us, which I did not mind because they actually make good holiday companions. My daughter often has very clear and sensible opinions about hotels. I think she actually might do well as a hotel reviewer. My son just loved being able to sleep in the same hotel room as his parents, because we always insisted that they sleep in their own bedrooms at home. There is no sense in being squashed every night in our bed by small people, in a house *we* pay for. In fact, I think it is a matter of life and death really. Doctors who do not sleep well are more likely to make mistakes that kill patients, so please excuse my parenting style.

This month, face coverings were made compulsory in shops, but thankfully not for children under 11 and people with certain medical conditions. I think most people had already accepted the need for wearing masks, but I was surprised to hear some people in a shop talking about how they did not like wearing masks because they thought masks cause eye and chest infections, and it is all a government conspiracy to make us all ill. Somehow, I struggled to see what the government had to gain by making us all ill and blocking up the limited hospital beds they were desperately trying to manage in this pandemic, but you dare not question the "word on the street" based on rumours started by people who think all professionals are liars.

I planned to keep working on a more trusting relationship with my own patients, so they can accept our public health advice and help change their friends' unhelpful health beliefs with time. This month, Public Health England warned that being obese or overweight was also a risk factor for severe illness or death with Covid-19. Obesity is a big problem, even among young people in England. Patient education was one big task for GPs in the Coronavirus pandemic, but I knew there was no other medical specialty better placed to do this. The relationship GPs build with their patients over years helps us to advise and reassure people more effectively in times like these. There were hopes of developing a new vaccine for Covid-19, and GPs were to be the main drivers of immunisation programmes whenever it became available. I sometimes felt overwhelmed at the thought of how much responsibility we have to the community as GPs, but I knew that we could get through it by working calmly together. GP surgeries had been delivering childhood immunisations and other vaccinations in the UK for years. All we needed was some good planning and the continued support of our excellent nurses and other healthcare colleagues to get this Coronavirus pandemic under control too.

I was excited to hear about the stamp duty holiday introduced by the government this month to help boost the housing market this year. There were still no viewings for our house, but I felt this was a good sign that it was time for us to move. The stamp duty holiday meant a saving of around £10,000 because there would be no stamp duty to pay to the government if we moved before March 2021. So many people were losing their jobs and being declined mortgages, but many others were seizing the opportunity to use the equity in their homes to get bigger houses and save on stamp duty. I wondered if the rising level of unemployment would reduce the number of people able to buy ours, but the reality was that we only needed *one* buyer. I genuinely wanted a nice family to buy ours, so our lovely neighbours would not have a hard time with someone new. The overall picture in the news was that the housing market was doing well, especially with this stamp duty incentive from the government. We just had to wait patiently for the right buyer. I was glad I had work and family to keep me busy while waiting.

My husband got the smallest cake for his birthday this month, because he does not really like cake, and we had eaten too much cake from May and June celebrations already. Whatever Christmas weight I had managed to shed was definitely back on by now. While others see an ever-slim woman, I can usually tell when I have an extra 2kg on me, so I made more effort to do my *Walk at Home* exercises five times a week this month. My husband came home just as I finished my walk in front of the television and joined us for dinner to celebrate his birthday. He joked about *Walk at Home* not being real exercise because I was not that sweaty, but my scales said otherwise. Burning more calories than you consume will lead to weight loss. Sounds like simple maths to me.

We surprised my husband with birthday messages from family and friends merged into one video, as was the popular thing for birthdays this year. My daughter even played the *Happy Birthday* song for him on her violin, which was beautiful to watch. What a lovely little lady she was becoming. We enjoyed his favourite rice meal and danced around the house with the children. It was hard to do something different for my husband, because Nigerian jollof rice and dancing were common occurrences in our home, and as he says "Why do something you don't like just to feel posh or special, when you are happy with what you have?". The man will gladly eat rice everyday, and is not as bothered about birthdays as I am. Thankfully, my husband's new signet ring was a perfect fit, but I got the feeling he preferred his good old gold wedding ring. This is one of the things I love about him. He is not materialistic or extravagant at all. I guess that's what men like him have a wife for, I thought, as I imagined my new sapphire ring.

The children had been talking about wanting a new play kitchen, so I checked out Facebook marketplace. It was beginning to feel like I was buying more toys than usual to make up for telling them we were moving, with no date in mind. I had to explain the "For Sale" sign and the significant decluttering they saw me do for viewings, so there was no way I could have hidden our plans from my clever children. Although I now think I could have tried harder to hide our moving plans from them, if I had known it would take this long to get a buyer. I often heard how houses were selling fast now that viewings had restarted, but still no news from our estate agent on ours. I finally found a cheap toy kitchen for the children, which bought me a few more weeks of distraction for them while we prayed for a buyer. It was beginning to look like we would be here for the start of school in September at this rate, which was not the ideal situation in my mind, but I chose to trust that things will happen at the right time for us.

We were all excited to visit Chesterfield on our way to Chatsworth House on our anniversary weekend. We booked a nice hotel near there, and prayed for good weather for our days out. We visited the famous Crooked Spire church in Chesterfield and enjoyed learning about its history. The children really enjoy eating at restaurants, and it was fun eating out each day in spite of the socially-distanced setup. Waiters had to leave food on the next table for us to collect, and we had to look at menus via apps on our phones to reduce contact. Who would have ever imagined eating out like this? One nice waiter kept coming back to our table to perform magic tricks for my children, which made their day. People who braved the outings this month enjoyed less crowded restaurants and more attention from the waiters, but we always had to book tables in advance.

We enjoyed a delicious picnic at Chatsworth House before it started to drizzle. I saw the rain as showers of blessing on our marriage. God has remained faithful throughout the years. He first told me to date/marry my husband through Chris Tomlin's song, *How great is our God*, at my church in Liverpool 15 years ago. God may not always give us exactly what we ask for, such as sunshine and trouble-free lives, but he always takes care of us when we follow His guidance for life. My husband was not the most eligible bachelor at university, but he turned out to be all I needed in a husband and much more. We had to buy a jumper from the Chatsworth House souvenir shop because the weather was cooler than we expected, but it turned out to be a lovely day out overall. The children kept saying how they wished our new house would be as big as Chatsworth House, with servants and horses. Sometimes I wonder how rich these children think we are. I would just be happy to have a detached house with a drive for two cars, but let's not limit God. If the children want a mansion, amen! Maybe we should cut down on the Disney movies too, I thought. My husband

and I always have great conversations on a long drive when the children fall asleep, so that made up a bit for the lack of privacy in our hotel room on our way back home. We were also grateful for our no-kids-in-our-bed policy when we came back!

My sapphire ring was as beautiful on my finger as I imagined. I had my nails done ready for anniversary morning when he placed it on my finger. I realised I too was still attached to my original gold wedding band, but it looked good with my new ring. I am probably just enjoying the freedom to wear precious stones after having to wear a plain wedding band in hospital jobs for years, due to infection control rules. I might grow out of this recent love of jewellery, but for now, I'm loving it! This anniversary present actually makes me smile on tough days. The little pleasures of life. True joy comes from Jesus, but as they say, whoever says money can't buy happiness does not know where to shop! At least, the big stone is always on my ring finger, so my patients do not have to worry when I have to do a digital rectal examination with my index finger in their bottom.

While working from home one morning, I spoke with a student who was feeling suicidal after finding out that she failed the final year of her university course. She had no past psychiatric history but she felt there was no one else she could talk to, hence the GP consultation. Her mother lived abroad and was openly disappointed that her daughter was still a student at 30. She told me how her mother often compared her to her younger brother who was already doing well as a doctor. My patient said that her closest friends lived in other cities, and she felt hopeless about her situation. I spent some time understanding her situation, assessing her suicide risk and signposted her to helpful mental health crisis services. She also agreed to get some overdue blood tests done that afternoon and see me at the surgery the next day. Sadly, seeing health professionals is sometimes all that some people have to look forward to in life.

She was on time for her face-to-face appointment with me the next day and opened up more about her struggles as an international student. By the end of the consultation, she felt more positive about her life and was empowered to submit an appeal against the university's decision with a supporting letter from her GP. We discussed the possible worst and best outcomes, and she was grateful. I reminded her also that she is an adult, and she can choose who she speaks to and when. If conversations with her mother were not helpful at certain times, she could be proactive at calling her mum herself when she felt strong, and end conversations when they got too negative. As much as we like to push our children to do well in their studies, it must not be at the expense of their mental health. I really do hope that my children do not one day feel the need to avoid me for the good of their mental health. Parenting is not easy, and I imagine parenting adults is an even tougher job that I will need God's help with.

For now, I will enjoy being able to laugh with my six-year-old daughter and four-year-old son, without the more complex issues of life on their minds. They usually ask us at the dinner table about our workday, and I am often impressed by their perspectives on certain issues. I know parents are warned not to compare their children, but mine make it hard not to. Thankfully, they are not both girls or boys, so I can sometimes blame the differences on gender. My girl was so keen to learn to read at four before she started school, but my boy initially couldn't care less. I bought him an easel so he could practice writing his name, at least, before September, and it seemed to encourage his interest in literacy. In lockdown, I realised he is actually very intelligent and capable when he decides to work. While people in other nations are fighting for education for the girl child, it is the boy child who needs to be convinced of his need for education in my house!

I was really hoping that my children could start in Reception and Year 2 at the Stratford School this September, but there were still no viewings booked for our house. House sales and purchases were taking around 12 weeks to complete, so even if we got a buyer now, we would not be in Stratford in time for the first day of school in September. I dreaded having to change their school in the middle of a school year, but I had now come to the conclusion that it would not be the worst thing. The children themselves were still very excited about moving, and I had confirmed that there were places for them in the relevant classes in the Stratford school I liked. Sadly, there were no places in Year 2 at the good school near the fenced house, so that helped me refocus and realise how crazy I was to want to send them to a school I had never even visited. The emotional ups and downs of the journey of moving house were worse than I imagined. I decided to just keep trusting God for His perfect timing and the right house.

As if they were put there to taunt me, so many houses in our village had “SOLD” signs this month. I sometimes had a little tantrum at God while driving down in my car. Please Father, let us sell now! I started thinking about what else I could do to help the situation. I got a quote for getting us a new driveway, in case that might improve our “curb appeal”, but I really did not have the motivation for any home improvements when my heart was already in Stratford. I decided to get other estate agents out to value our house for different opinions as to why it was not getting any viewings. They all kept saying how beautiful our house was, how well the housing market was doing and how we might need to drop the price to sell fast in the pandemic. Of course, anything would sell if you advertised it for cheap. We were not ready to drop the price, especially now that we had missed the September school start deadline I wanted to beat. We needed to sell for a reasonable price to be able to afford a nice house in Stratford-upon-Avon anyway.

The agent selling our "dream house" in Stratford was very proactive. He would often call to check how we were getting on with our sale, so he could update his client. This was before it was sold to the other buyer. I wondered why no one was calling me with a weekly update too. The straw that broke the camel's back was when I called him to request a viewing for a similar property listed that morning on Rightmove, and he told me that it was already sold! He said that they only listed it on Rightmove to gauge other interest. Why didn't anyone sell mine that quickly with offline marketing?! This was when I suggested to my husband that we should try another estate agent at the end of this month, when our contract with the current agent ended. I also hoped that listing with a new agent would give our house advert a boost, with new photos and alerts on Rightmove. I hated feeling desperate, but I also looked up a "sell your house quick" company and found one that did not seem as dodgy as the others. I was still not desperate enough for new build part exchanges though, probably because there were no new builds near the school I liked.

As my son was not able to have his nursery "graduation" photos taken as expected this year, we booked a photoshoot with a new photographer who was advertising Back to School mini photoshoots for children who missed out on graduation ceremonies due to Covid-19. I was so proud to see him in that little graduation gown. I remember thinking how silly these graduation ceremonies for four-year-olds are, until I had my own children. It is truly a lot to celebrate when they are ready for school, without nappies and milk, speaking clearly and using their manners. Seemed like yesterday when we were carrying them in car seats, and now they are able to get dressed independently. I never take their good health and development for granted, knowing as a doctor how many things can go wrong even in the first four years of life. God has been really good to us. My son was so easygoing as a baby - as if he knew he was a second child. It was hard to believe we were now teaching him to read using phonics:

"What sound is this?"

"C"

"Go on.."

"C-A-T"

"And what does that make?"

"Boy"

What?! I realised he was trying to guess the words from the photos on each page, instead of blending in the sounds he had learned. My daughter would get frustrated and find another book to read by herself whenever it was his turn to read at bedtime. I am glad he eventually made progress and is now reading well. Big thumbs up to those very patient school teachers that work with children everyday.

The children had successful "transition days" at our village school before the start of the summer holidays this month. I, on the other hand, struggled to engage with all the new parent activities for Reception class because I had done it all before with my daughter - I was even the Parent Teacher Association (PTA) Reception class representative in her time. I was secretly hoping we would be able to do Reception this time for my son in Stratford.

We spent some of the summer holidays viewing more houses in Stratford, and I wondered how many other people view houses with no intention to buy them. We even considered going for a smaller house with the potential to extend, but decided against it after a few viewings of some smaller houses. This made me really appreciate the space we have in ours, especially after turning it into one with a nice open plan kitchen. Our house seemed like the kind of house that would sell fast, especially with the fantastic choice of colours, if I may say so myself. Actually, a lot of people told us it would sell fast, including estate agents. This was probably why I was getting frustrated. There can only be one answer when things like this happen to me. It must be that God has a better plan than mine, and I just had to wait.

I took my husband to see a three-bedroom house near the fenced house I liked, but he was not keen. It was near the school with no Year 2 spaces, so it was not actually a good idea anyway. I realised my standards were dropping a bit during the wait. When my husband said he did not want it, I knew he was right. That was not the kind of house we wanted. Besides, we had prayed for a four-bedroom house, because we like having a guest room. God kindly reminded me through the Bible verse I read that day that His plans for me are for good (Jeremiah 29:11), so there was no need to aim lower in desperation. I love how God is patient with us, even when we seem to forget how good He is, and all He has done before.

I was still looking on Rightmove everyday, and hoping another great house would come up near my favourite school. Finally, I agreed to see one that my husband had pointed out before. It was a four-bedroom house that needed a lot of renovation. I wanted a house on a close, but this was on an avenue and only five minutes' walk from the school. I fell in love with it when we got to see it. It was funny to me that the agent had refused to show it to my husband when he contacted them to request a viewing earlier this year, but we got a viewing quickly when he called again after I agreed to give it a chance.

It might have been a combination of different factors that made us get a viewing appointment this time, but this little incident reminded me of the power of unity in marriage. We achieve a lot more in the physical as married couples when we are united in spirit. This principle has also worked well for our finances too. We are still growing in this area. Husbands and wives can achieve more with their income when they are open with each other and plan together on how best to use their money together as one family. One of the prophecies we were given for our wedding was that we would become a multiplication of both, not just the sum of two. I believe this is God's will for every marriage, when we have Jesus as our solid foundation. For those who are not yet married and hoping to do so one day, remember that there will be nothing to multiply if you do not use this time to invest in your personal growth and development, so that you can be a blessing to your spouse and the world. God has a great plan for your life, whether married or not. As one preacher used to say, incomplete people end up having an incomplete marriage, so do not wait for marriage to complete you.

The house we saw needed less renovation than I imagined. I could already see myself picking out the new kitchen and redesigning the garden. It was advertised for less than our budget because of the need for renovations and I thought that was a good sign, until I noticed some cracks on the walls. My husband immediately switched off at this, but I was still optimistic and phoned around for quotes for repair in the worst-case scenario. I also asked the seller's estate agent to get details of the problem for us from the owner.

I was disappointed to hear that the cracks were due to drainage problems which can be very expensive to fix, but I tried to stay positive and let them know we might still be interested if the price was further reduced in the light of this. Thankfully, our house still did not sell, so we did not have to make a serious decision about buying this. Looking back now, I think this was another period of impatience that could have led to big financial troubles, if God had not delayed our house sale. I was a bit jealous of my husband's calmness about this issue, and we even had "words" about his recent laid back attitude towards the house move. "Words" turned into "loud sentences" when he suggested that we forget the house move for now. What?! I'm not a quitter!! No!!!

It is sometimes hard to know when to keep pushing for something and when to stop. Christians sometimes talk about P.U.S.H. = Pray Until Something Happens. I value the oneness we have in our marriage when making decisions. I did not want to force my way as the beloved, influential wife. What we both wanted was God's will. This is when I realised I needed to spend some time alone with God about this. I am normally very strong in the face of challenges, but this was a totally different ball game, because it felt like a challenge I chose. It was not a *need*, per se. We did not have to move. We could easily stay here another ten years and life would not be bad. We had lovely neighbours and good schools here. Why did I have this strong motivation to move? Why would God put this desire in our hearts and let us struggle?

One of our Christian friends even asked if God had specifically told us to move. I secretly wanted to ask if God had told him to have breakfast. Every Christian knows how they hear from God personally, and I knew what it was for me, but that question sort of bothered me. I had to spend time away from Stratford, Rightmove, friends and common sense to know what God was saying concerning this matter at this time. Our business plans were also being stalled by the delayed approval from NHS England. That was one of the reasons why we wanted to move to Stratford, and the delay with that was discouraging my husband too. I took Friday off work and spent more time with God that weekend through fasting and prayer with my husband. Although I lost my excess tummy and the desperation, I did not hear the loud voice from heaven that people sometimes hope to hear. God spoke quietly in my spirit reminding me that He put the desires in our hearts and will work it out in His own time. I had a fresh experience of God's powerful love for me, and felt okay to carry on without knowing the exact details of His plan. I just had to trust Him, as it says in one of my favourite childhood memory verses from the Bible, Proverbs 3:5,6 - *Trust in the Lord with all your heart and do not rely on your own understanding. In all your ways acknowledge Him and He will direct your paths*. That was exactly what I needed, so I could proceed from a place of peace, not desperation. We did not need to worry about how the delay made us look. We just needed to be obedient and Christ-centred at every step of the journey, even if it made us look stupid. If we can all wear masks and stay at home for a virus we cannot see, surely we can trust an invisible God who has done greater things before. This Christian walk is truly by faith and not by sight (2 Corinthians 5:7).

Meanwhile, I was chosen randomly to receive a Covid-19 testing kit by post. It was not pleasant getting the test sample from my nose and throat, but thank God the result was negative. My Covid-19 antibody test at work, which was now available for healthcare workers, also came back negative, which was neither here nor there, because at this point it was not clear whether a positive antibody test meant immunity anyway. I was very grateful for the hardworking scientists trying to get us answers, and prayed that we would be free of this pandemic soon. People were still losing jobs and businesses, including those in the performing arts and events sector. People who had only known music their whole lives were having to think of ways to retrain for other jobs to pay their bills. I heard a classical musician speaking on the radio about how she had to work on a farm to make ends meet because of all the cancelled events in lockdown. A young wedding photographer had also started studying online for a degree, which sounded like a good way to turn the challenge of lockdown into an opportunity for better qualifications and options for the future.

At the end of the month, I received an electronic estate agent contract from the less dodgy quick house sale company I was speaking to, but I was not happy with some of the points there. They insisted the points on the contract could not be changed even though they understood my concerns, so we refused to sign it. We decided to go with an estate agent recommended by the very proactive agent in Stratford. I insisted on an eight-week sole agent contract, instead of the usual 12, because I did not want to be stuck with one agent for another three months if they were not being proactive enough to sell our house. The stamp duty holiday was due to end in March 2021, so I calculated that we had to agree to a sale by November at the latest to take advantage of this, if it was for us. I am sure that God can provide all we need to move house at another time without this incentive, if He wants to. He owns the whole world! The new estate agent was polite and came promptly to take photos of our house, ready to list it on Rightmove etc as soon as our contract expired in August. This time, I felt peaceful and trusted God's will to be done concerning the timing of our house sale.

Matthew 6:33-34
But seek first His kingdom and His righteousness, and all these things will be given to you as well. Therefore do not worry about tomorrow, for tomorrow will worry about itself. Each day has enough trouble of its own.

Chapter 8
AUGUST
Dream house

The summer holidays had started, but there was no real break from work for my children because they usually did educational activities in the mornings while I did my consultations. They sometimes had to come into work with me, and do some colouring in the lovely Practice Manager's office due to lack of summer childcare in the pandemic. I just hoped the over-exposure to healthcare settings at a young age would not kill my daughter's interest in medicine. I was pleased when she told me one day that she would have a much nicer office than mine when she became a doctor. Although I sometimes felt that it would be better for her to explore an easier life outside medicine! We were all looking forward to moving into the new purpose-built surgery in 2021. With the tiny room I currently used, I imagined some tax collectors in Jesus' day probably had nicer offices.

Our annual summer Bible Week for church was cancelled last month due to the pandemic. It was meant to be a big one in 2020, as we were celebrating the 50th year of Bible Week. It was usually a week of camping, prayer, worship, Bible seminars, games and sharing amazing testimonies of all God was doing through our churches around the world. It was also a great time to catch up with Christian friends from churches in other cities. We used to go for just the weekend meetings when we first got married, but it has been great to be able to attend for the whole week in recent years. Our children loved it, especially because it was fun for them to stay with us in a hotel room for five nights. Other families enjoyed camping together on the site, but after my first (and last) experience of camping in 2011, it would take God's intervention to get me to do it again!

Seriously though, I think about my life and think how blessed we are. Even when things do not go how we plan, it is really not that bad. Having to sleep in a cold tent for a few nights would be a small sacrifice to pay in obedience to God, if that is what He really wanted me to do. This month I watched an old documentary called *Beyond the gates of splendour* on Youtube about five American missionaries who felt led by God to share the gospel of Jesus with people in a jungle tribe that were known for killing people, even their own - using spears! After investing so much to build trust and friendship, the villagers eventually killed all five of them after a little misunderstanding. The missionaries had guns to defend themselves, but I was so touched by the fact that they promised themselves that they would never harm those people, whatever happened. These men had wives and small children to worry about, but they chose to trust God and give their lives to reach others with the good news of salvation through Jesus. They let themselves be speared to death instead of killing the villagers, because they were sure of their future in heaven, but "the villagers were not yet ready to meet God".

What was so amazing was the reality of how God really turns situations around for good. When we stop focusing so much on ourselves and try to see things from a greater heavenly perspective, we can see that truly, all things work together for good. The wives and children of these men impressively stayed back to continue the mission, and eventually led the villagers to faith in Jesus. Tears filled my eyes when I saw how one of the killers had become like a grandfather to one of the American children, after he became a Christian. He even visited America for the boy's graduation years later. The young man mentioned how having his father killed there actually helped him to fit in, because most of the other children were fatherless too through spear deaths in the village. The courage of those men to bring the good news about life in Jesus to that place led to a change in the culture and a safer environment for many generations.

We often ask "Why me?" when something bad happens. I have never heard anyone seriously ask the same question when something good happens to them. As if it is our right to have a nice life, while others suffer instead? This is a broken, sinful world where pain and sorrow abound. As a Christian, I am aware that Jesus never promised us a trouble-free life, but He promised that He would never leave us. He has indeed made us more than conquerors, as it says in Romans 8 - one of my favourite chapters of the Bible. The little problems of selling and buying a house quickly seemed like nothing in comparison to the trials these people faced as Christians who were also living for Jesus. God is more interested in our spiritual growth than in the little comforts we crave, but He cares enough also to hear our prayers for the little things like hotel rooms instead of camping, and a house in Stratford near great schools. Who knows what else God is accomplishing through this 2020 experience - for us and others watching us. I just prayed that I would never be too distracted by the gifts that I forget the Giver.

August was a very busy month for me at work because I had to cover several on-call sessions for colleagues taking well-deserved annual leave. Even though General Practice can sometimes seem a lot like lone working, there was still camaraderie and teamwork. Doing these pre-arranged extra GP on-call cover sessions was still better for me than junior doctor hospital posts where I just got given a rota with random hours to work with. I had to try to swap some weekend on-call shifts with doctors I had probably never spoken to before, so I could have a tiny bit of a social life and maintain my sanity then. All that hard work was paying off now, and I loved being able to choose when I work. Even the worst days in GP were not that bad, in my opinion. I guess that is a sign of being in the right specialty. This month, we had a lot of anxious patients calling for doctor's notes because they were worried about going back to work after shielding or working from home for months. The human mind is amazing. First, we were dreading staying at home for lockdown, now people were comfortable at home and did not want to go back to work.

My children became very good at keeping quiet when I was doing phone consultations. They would usually only speak to me after I hung up. I was impressed with their sensibility at this age, although they sometimes asked me "How many more patients?" too many times. Bless them. Thankfully, the government confirmed this month that schools would resume in September and they urged parents to send their children. Of course, this was another source of anxiety because people were worried about having their precious babies sitting next to children of hospital workers. Some children were so out of routine with school that we also had to deal with the anxieties around returning for young people themselves. Anxiety presented in different ways, for example, women saying that their children had breathing problems, or men complaining about a constant lump in the throat. Patients do not always list symptoms precisely as stated in medical textbooks, so that we can give a quick diagnosis. GPs are often the ones who get the first phone call about the problem when their symptoms are still quite vague. We have to sieve through the context of the problem and the layman descriptions to get to the serious diagnosis, if any. Some of the patients I brought in for face-to-face consultations mainly needed to have an examination for reassurance. They were mostly children of worried mothers.

Amongst all this, we also had to be vigilant for people with serious problems who needed urgent referrals and cancer investigations. I remember seeing a lady who had a rapid decline in neurological symptoms over lockdown. She was an active businesswoman in January, but she was now needing help to walk and talk. She kept minimising her symptoms, and could have easily been dismissed as still suffering from the impact of a road traffic accident she had been involved in last year. Something about the telephone consultation did not feel right, so I asked her to come in. I was surprised at how unwell she was when she came in using a stick and leaning on her teenage daughter. Her speech was also difficult to understand. I sent an urgent neurology referral with her consent, and took time to explain my examination findings and concerns to the patient and her family. I phoned them to follow up a week later, and heard that she had received a hospital appointment to be reviewed in 2 months' time. Hospitals were struggling to keep up with non-Covid patients in the pandemic. Many planned operations and clinic appointments were unfortunately postponed as a result. I knew my hospital colleagues were doing their best with limited resources, but this patient was deteriorating fast, and now struggling to swallow. After several phone calls to hospital colleagues to get her seen that week, her husband later told me that they decided not to go to the earlier appointment I arranged because they were worried about catching Coronavirus in hospital! That was a big lesson for me in confirming what the patient really wanted to do about their problem, before going out of my way to solve it. Thankfully, we were able to offer her other support in the community before she had her telephone consultation with the neurology consultant.

It was now two weeks into our contract with the new (recommended) estate agent, but no news. They had no viewings booked and hardly replied to my emails! I tried not to be too pushy, because they were recommended by that good estate agent in Stratford, but I also did not want to waste more time. After a few phone calls, they finally told me that they had a viewing booked for our house. Thankfully, I had the names of potential buyers who viewed or tried to view our house with the previous agent. I was not pleased to see that the viewing they had booked was someone who had already tried to view our house with the previous agent. If she wanted to buy our house, we might have to pay agent fees to two agents. I agreed to the viewing anyway - it was better than nothing.

My children must have thought I was crazy when preparing for a viewing. The house had to look like a showhome. With most toys put away and decluttering done, they had to sit still, so they would not make a mess before going out. Sitting still for 20 minutes is like standing on one leg for ten hours to my children. They grumbled about not being able to bring toys downstairs or play in the garden while I got the last bits done ready to go out. They sometimes got some nice treats while out - to ease my conscience mainly. It usually took them only 20 minutes to turn the house back into a "family home" when we returned after a viewing. I was sometimes surprised at how little effort some people put into preparing their houses for viewings when we went to see some ourselves, but I was not about to let a bit of clutter put off my potential buyer. We keenly waited for feedback the next day, and my daughter kept showing me photos of what she wanted her new room at our next house to look like.

You can imagine my surprise and annoyance when the estate agent told me the next day that the lady never showed up to view the house! I was not sure who to be more upset with - the agent or the lady. At least the agent could have told me this before he left our house that day when the lady didn't show up. This added to their list of crimes for poor communication. It took so much strength for me to agree to get the house ready again for another viewing with this lady some weeks later with this agent, only for her to tell them that the house was too big for her. There were dimensions and photos of the house on Rightmove, for goodness' sake! Anyway, I was glad she was not buying it, because I really did not want to have to pay commission to two agents for her sake. I calmed down and was reminded of the Bible passage below. We find rest in God when we remember that there is more to success than human effort. The key to success is really in the hands of the Master of the Universe, who loves us.

Psalm 127.1-2
Unless the Lord builds the house,
the builders labour in vain.
Unless the Lord watches over the city,
the guards stand watch in vain.
In vain you rise early and stay up late,
toiling for food to eat - for He grants sleep
to those He loves.

We enjoyed the government *Eat Out to Help Out* scheme this month, which was a good distraction from the lack of viewings and busyness of GP work. As restaurants had now reopened and the government was trying to boost the economy, people could eat at participating restaurants on certain days of the week for half the usual cost. A bargain-lover like me had to try this, especially as eating out is one of our favourite things to do as a family. I booked tables at a few restaurants we liked throughout the month, so there was something to look forward to every week. The children and I enjoyed desserts at a gelato place in Coventry and a Stratford pub lunch on days when their father was at work. This popular pub was only a few minutes away from the houses we liked. I could imagine having some lovely summer afternoons there when we finally moved to Stratford.

I stayed up late a few nights looking at houses and floor plans on Rightmove. Dreams are free - I would happily fantasise about any house I liked, even without a buyer for mine, because I know God can do anything. Sometimes we worry about a problem for ages and suddenly God changes the situation, and we wonder why we spent time worrying. Instead of worrying, I like to enjoy thinking about solutions and dreaming of better times. My husband always finds it ridiculous that I make plans for things not yet confirmed. He wonders how I can quickly overcome the disappointment if it does not happen, and move on to new dreams. I guess it is a coping mechanism, and I certainly find it less stressful than expecting the worst. After all, "faith is the assurance of things not seen", so I am usually prepared for my answered prayers.

I was disappointed again when the Stratford agent told me that the cracked house I was considering had sold, and we still had no viewings for ours. I was beginning to get angry with this new estate agent, who seemed more lazy than proactive to me. Do they just list houses on Rightmove, hope it sells and get a commission? No wonder they were so keen to get us signed on, then seemed to forget about us after we joined their agency. I was not seeing evidence of any active marketing, and no one was calling to update me on how it was going - whether good or bad. Maybe I was expecting too much. Some friends told me how their houses took a year to sell, but I refused to believe that it was a matter of chance, otherwise, why are we offering the agents so much commission? God kept reminding me that He is in control and will provide the right house at the right time. I just needed to stay in peace. Psalm 23 reminded me that being in the "House of the Lord all the days of my life" was more important than my postcode.

Psalm 23

The Lord is my shepherd, I lack nothing.
He makes me lie down in green pastures,
He leads me beside quiet waters,
He refreshes my soul.
He guides me along the right paths
    for His name's sake.
Even though I walk
    through the darkest valley
I will fear no evil,

for you are with me;
your rod and your staff,
they comfort me.
You prepare a table before me
in the presence of my enemies.
You anoint my head with oil;
my cup overflows.
Surely your goodness and love will follow me
all the days of my life,
and I will dwell in the house of the Lord
forever.

The Bible is the only book you read where the Author speaks at the same time to you through His Holy Spirit. I was so grateful for such powerful words to keep me going on difficult days in 2020. I was also excited to get a phone call a few days later from the really proactive agent in Stratford telling me that our original "dream house" was now back on the market! This is the house we made an offer on, which later sold to another buyer who sold their house before us. I was not happy that someone's house sale fell through, but it just made me remember that nothing is impossible with God. I did not need to have a formula or force my way to get anything. What is mine will be mine, whether this house or another. It was such a good faith boost and motivation to keep waiting for our right buyer at the right time. Miracles do happen. And, like Shadrach, Meshach and Abednego said about serving only the one true God even if He did not deliver them from the fiery furnace (Daniel 3), I will trust God even if He decides not to give us a new house at all.

For my blog this month, I wrote an article with my six-year-old daughter about returning to school in September. I was impressed by her wisdom and contribution. She told other children to focus on the fact that they would get to see their friends and teachers when school resumed. Even though I wanted my son to start school in Stratford so we would not have to change in the middle of the school year, I was happy that he would get to see his nursery friends in school, while we were still living in our village. He had missed his best friend over the break, and being here meant that they would share the experience of starting school together. Indeed, all things work together for our good, and God knows what is more important for our future. It is sometimes so hard to believe this though, especially when we want something sorted now, AS.A.P, today. Sometimes the good being worked out might be the greater good for God's kingdom, and as children of God, it is an honour to be instruments in the hands of our Maker. We had several opportunities to show God's love to our friends and neighbours in the village this year which we might not have had if we moved earlier as planned.

Another good email came this month from NHS England in response to the complaint they received about me and the practice earlier this year. Our Practice Manager forwarded their response in which they apologised for taking longer than usual to get back to us. I was glad I did not waste time fretting about this, and got lots done in the meantime. The NHS complaints officer did some investigations and concluded that what I did was right for the patient, and supported the surgery's decision not to tolerate abuse to staff. This boosted my confidence in the system, even though I reflected a lot on what else I could have done to get a better outcome from the consultation. I do not want to be a GP who gives patients whatever they want for a quiet life. I want to help them see why I refuse to do what they want when I have to say no. I have since brushed up on this skill, or maybe the patients here have had time to get to know and trust me better. I was not completely happy with NHS England on a personal level though, because we were still waiting for their response to the application we made months ago for approval for my husband to start the healthcare business he was buying. Lockdown caused significant delays to our plans for entrepreneurship, but we decided to trust God with the timing of this too. The ups and downs from this entrepreneurial aspect of our year would be enough to write another book, but God's peace kept us sane through it all.

It can sometimes be tempting to become proud or feel frustrated in professions like medicine, especially in some of the deprived communities we serve, so I try to remind myself regularly that God gave me this job and career as another avenue to serve Him. I do not want to take that for granted. On difficult days, I often look at a Bible verse in my office reminding me that "*Even the Son of Man did not come to be served, but to serve, and to give his life as a ransom for many.*" (Mark 10.45) Who then am I to not serve others, when Jesus, the Son of God, Almighty God Himself, chose to serve humanity and even laid down His life for us? All we are is by God's grace, and remembering that keeps me humble as a doctor.

Our shopping for school was almost done. I just needed to get a few shirts for my son. I tried not to buy too many white shirts because I hoped that they would not need them after this term when they transferred to their new school. I loved the Stratford school uniform colours, and could not wait to see my children in them. It is amazing what little silly things matter to mothers. I hoped my children would still be able to enjoy their friendships in our village school, even though many people knew we were planning to move. I hoped they would like their teachers, but not so much that moving would be a problem. I hoped they and their bubbles would stay well, so I did not have to keep them home for two weeks in term time. I am not a worrier, but there was still so much to worry about if I let myself, so I left it all to God. He will take care of them and bring us whatever help we need at every stage. I thank God that He has indeed never failed us, even in a pandemic.

After spending so much time with the children during the week, I looked forward to my Saturday morning Extended Access GP sessions, which I recently started doing again. They were also mostly telephone consultations, which I was paid an hourly rate for as a locum, because it was outside my normal salaried GP role. I felt it would be too lazy not to do any, considering the fact that I actually enjoyed those sessions and could save the money towards the new house. It was also a good three hours where I could hear myself think between patients, because my husband was home with our children. I still don't know how I managed to spend almost every waking hour with my children during the summer holidays. It has definitely been a year of plenty of grace and strength from Jesus.

There was no going to work for a break, because they had to come with me. I was doubly sure after this summer that "my quiver is full" with two children (Psalm 127). Imagine the chaos if I had to bring more than two children into work with me regularly. I often joke that my other two children are being raised by my children's future in-laws.

Just when you think you know what you want, you meet that amazing baby at work that makes you want to have babies again. I have the privilege of doing postnatal checks for new mums and examining their babies at about two months old when they come for their first immunisations. Today's baby was one I could have easily taken home with me. She was so beautiful and content, I had to tell my ovaries to stop screaming! This is the joy of "cradle to grave" care in General Practice. I could easily be doing a postnatal check on this baby's baby in 30 years time, if I kept working here. Wow! Sadly in the same week, I found out that a lady whom I had supported through her journey with the fertility clinic while trying to conceive had just miscarried the pregnancy we recently celebrated. I could not even begin to imagine how she felt, because my own emotions took me weeks to process. Sometimes things happen that we just have no explanation for, in spite of our prayers and efforts. All I could do was to trust

God to comfort her and give me wisdom to be a helpful GP at this time, and He did. I choose to thank Him *in* all things as the Bible says, even if not *for* all things (1 Thessalonians 5:18).

Thankfully, the government's school reopening plans continued, and my son could not wait to start school, so he could have a break from my job! We might have had to get them real jobs at the surgery, if they did not stop coming with me. My children missed being able to go abroad this summer, but they were looking forward to the charity trip to Lagos in October. These children actually love flying. Even though I wanted to do the charity trip in time for the Coventry City of Culture 2021 celebration we won the award for, it still did not feel safe enough to travel with the children this year, and I did not want to leave it too late to change plans. By now, we had sorted a venue for our Lagos seminars through my sister-in-law. The Lagos school her children went to was happy to host us. Why did I not think to ask her sooner? At least, the venue was one less thing to worry about now. I pondered for weeks and finally decided after discussion with my husband and charity trustees that it was best to postpone the Lagos trip to 2021. There goes another three hours of my life waiting on hold to speak to airline agents to be able to change our travel dates without paying more than double the original ticket prices.

My children were disappointed when I told them that I had now moved the travel dates to 2021, but I could not imagine us enjoying a six-hour flight wearing masks next to other anxious passengers in a pandemic. I was grateful that we actually visited Lagos on our last trip to Nigeria as a family, after my sister's wedding in Kaduna, so there was no rush to go back. As the Bible says, there is time for everything (Ecclesiastes 3). This could be a really impactful and memorable one week in Lagos with good timing, but bad timing could easily make it our last trip to Nigeria. I decided to book a nice consolation trip for my children in England. Despite my initial lack of fondness for Peppa Pig (children's show) before having my own children, I booked a trip to Peppa Pig World for the end of the summer holidays as a treat for the children before school starts. Any pig that makes them sit quietly while I do my work, is a good pig in my books.

We saw a few more houses in Stratford this weekend and drove by the "dream house" again, because my daughter had her first face-to-face violin lesson since March with her Stratford-based music teacher. Zoom lessons worked well, but it was better to have a proper music lesson in person while keeping our distance from each other. Visiting Stratford again this weekend made us even more convinced that we wanted to live there. The proximity to his future work location for the new business was a great perk for my husband, and we loved the town centre. My children really enjoyed the boat rides there. After renting different types of houses as international students years ago, we knew exactly what kind of houses we liked. All our showhome visits and travelling experience also helped. The recent house viewings convinced us about the types of houses and locations we definitely did not want. It seems funny now to think that there was a time my husband and I used to look at showhomes as a fun thing to do on weekends. Now I was tired of viewing houses with a face covering, and just wanted to move.

Our current estate agent had only arranged one other viewing apart from the one for the prospective buyer introduced by the previous agent. I was not happy at all. A grand total of four viewings since March! No wonder we had no buyer. If the statistics were right, we needed to have around ten viewings for one offer. Conversations with the estate agent about how best to move forward were always initiated by me, after several attempts to contact them. I wondered if they were missing potential buyers with their poor response to phone calls and emails. There was a bit of an improvement in communication after I gave them a 3/10 score on their head office feedback request. Now, I could not wait for the contract to be over so I could sell the house myself, because I did not feel they deserved any commission when it was sold. I had an idea to make my own PDF brochure of the house and send it to friends who might be able to spread the word and get us a buyer that way. I try not to ignore ideas that come into my head, because they just could be answers to prayers. We had one viewing from that idea, but no offer. At least, I felt I was doing something about the situation, and no worse than the current agent.

Finally, I could have my birthday dinner with my May-born friends, as planned. We caught up on work and mum-life stories. One of them was also planning to move to Stratford from Coventry, so we talked about the pros and cons for our children. It was lovely to catch up over dinner without our husbands and children. GPs can sometimes be the dumping ground for other people's problems. People get constipated with life's issues and flush it all down our ears in a ten-minute consultation, which sometimes needs a prescription like toilet paper to clean up the mess. It is a privilege to be able to help in that way, but even toilets need a good clean sometimes. Being able to relax and unwind with like-minded women outside of work was definitely something I missed during lockdown.

It was soon the last weekend of August. We got our hair done ready for the new term. Even my son had a new haircut for the first day of school. We were so glad to have the salons open again. I was particularly pleased to be able to sort out my bushy eyebrows after poor attempts at home grooming for months. My husband, like the rest of us, was looking forward to our August weekend away because he worked very hard this summer on the frontline. We booked a hotel near a beach in Bournemouth, and visited friends and family while down south. We were all used to the outdoor/garden socially-distanced visits these days due to Coronavirus restrictions.

We had one last *Eat Out to Help Out* discounted meal in Salisbury on our way back home, and saw the famous Magna Carta at the Salisbury Cathedral. It was a lovely experience, in spite of social distancing. The children loved their time at the beach and the rides at Peppa Pig World. The weather was perfect. I like to show our children the benefits of hard work and make them realise that their being sensible and patient with us while we work allows us to be able to have such nice little holidays with them. It is all by God's grace, but the principles of sowing and reaping cannot be ignored. You harvest what you plant. I hope that they also learn to work hard themselves from their youth, so that they can have better options as adults for a good life. This is especially important for our princess daughter, who thought our Bournemouth hotel was not quite good enough for her. Rest is good, but this Bible verse often makes us laugh and jump out of bed on lazy days.

Proverbs 24:33
A little sleep, a little slumber, a little folding of the hands to rest—and poverty will come on you like a thief and scarcity like an armed man.

Chapter 9
SEPTEMBER
Second wave

I was so excited to finally have both my children in school, and at the same school. It made dropping them off in the mornings easier, but I still thought they could do with personal secretaries! There was so much information to keep up with for each class: what day to wear or bring what, PTA fundraising events, termly learning conferences not to be missed, school apps to download, homework activities, optional extras etc. I am amazed at how mothers cope with more than two children and their activities. On the brighter side, our dinner conversations went up another level. It was great to hear the same story from the perspectives of two different children:

"Today, my teacher said 'Well done' to me, but I don't remember what it was for."

"That's good! I'm glad you are doing well in school, Son. How was your day, lovely girl?"

"It was good. The headteacher *recognised* me."

"Wow! What was that for?"

"I don't know - she just said that she recognised 'all of us' at the school assembly, and that includes me."

"That's great!" I said, trying to hide a chuckle. "So, which teacher did you have today?"

"Mrs. Brown"

"How about you, Son? What was your teacher's name?"

"I don't know, but it started with Mrs."

That's how much information you get from the boy, compared to the girl who knew every single Reception teacher's name in her first week of school. At least, my son thought school was "Awesome", which was definitely an answered prayer considering national anxieties around going back to school properly after lockdown, with rising Coronavirus infection rates. The NHS Test and Trace programme was struggling because of high demand for Covid-19 tests, with some people having to travel long distances to get tested. There were concerns about a second peak of infection rates as university students prepared to return too. We hoped there would not be a second peak, but some predicted it was inevitable with schools and universities resuming.

We tried to make the first day of school as nice for my son as it was for my daughter, but God made it even more special. I am glad God does not show "firstborn bias", like us imperfect parents. It is funny to see how enthusiasm for firsts often declines with subsequent children in our flawed parenting. We've been there, done that, but we need to remember that this particular child hasn't. My husband was unexpectedly without work that week in preparation for his new job, for which the start date was delayed due to unexpected delays in NHS England approval for the new business. Our children were so pleased to have Daddy available to pick them up on some days after school in the first week. I remember the disappointed look I got from my son one day when I turned up after his father had promised to pick him up. I have now learned my lesson to go only where I am wanted.

As my husband is self-employed, he gets paid only for the days he works - no sick pay or annual leave pay. We hoped that the transition from his old locum job contract to the new one would be seamless, but lockdown had led to this no-income situation we hoped could be avoided. He decided to intentionally take the first week of September off to rest and enjoy the start of the new term with the family, but we both prayed he would find work soon, so we did not have to start diving into our savings. Some of my GP friends' husbands had sadly lost their jobs this year, and I knew the financial stress this could cause if both salaries were required to run the house. In the first week of September, there was no sign of any work for my husband, but we chose to trust that God would provide all we needed. At least we had some savings, but even that could disappear in a few months if household income is halved. There would be no more talk of a new house, and we would have to cut down on other expenses. It is so easy for our minds to wander off and worry about the worst, but God's peace remained with us in this season, reminding us that He is our source and strength.

Philippians 4:12-13
I know what it is to be in need, and I know what it is to have plenty. I have learned the secret of being content in any and every situation, whether well fed or hungry, whether living in plenty or in want. I can do all this through Him who gives me strength.

My husband and I have experienced being broke and in plenty, but we also know how to be content in every situation. Contentment does not mean lack of ambition, laziness or pride. As Christians, we live in God's economy and He is our faithful provider. He saw us through tough times in the past and we knew He could do it again, if it ever came to that. God supplies our needs "according to the riches of His glory in Christ Jesus" (Phillipians 4:19), not according to national GDP or current salary. Tommy Walker's song, *We will remember* was a great comfort and reminder to me in this season. When we think back on all God has done for us, we find strength to believe for all He will do.

At the school gates this month, we met a few "lockdown babies" (as we called them). Their mums would have been in their first trimester when we last saw them, stayed indoors for the big tummy phase, and have now appeared looking great with new babies in September. Children are such a blessing. I was excited knowing that my newlywed sister in Nigeria was expecting a baby too. If only having a baby was as easy as it looked from afar. This year, many pregnant women had to be seen on their own by healthcare professionals due to Covid-19 restrictions. Having a partner there for the antenatal appointments and birth became a luxury to be missed. Women had to be strong for themselves and their families. Those with older children struggled even more because they could not have anyone babysit during lockdown, so the pregnant mother had to go into hospital on her own in labour. I remember how blessed I was to have my husband with me for the births of both our children, and can only imagine how difficult it must have been for these new mums. All people see now is a beautiful lockdown baby who seemed to just appear from nowhere in the craziness of 2020. I was happy to see that these people came through the difficulties as families. I realised that even though I was not physically pregnant in 2020, I would eventually have my birth of 2020 dreams, in spite of lockdown, by God's grace. I just need to always remember that the timing (as with childbirth labour) is in God's hands, not mine.

I now heard of my friends putting their houses on the market too - they were selling and having offers accepted on new homes. Why was nothing happening on our side? There were still no viewings and we were still tied into an eight-week contract with the agent recommended by the Stratford estate agent. Our estate agent suggested bringing down our asking price, so we agreed to reduce it a bit this time. According to the news, house prices were going up, so I was not convinced that our price was the issue, especially if there was no one actively marketing the property, but we had to give their idea a chance. Our "dream house" was still available, and we were the only ones who had an offer on it so far. I also called to confirm that places were still available for my children at the nearby school I liked. This was all reassuring, but I still had to be patient when nothing seemed to be happening for our house sale. My son told me that the best thing about his first day at school was seeing his best friend there, which somehow made the delay worth it. I reminded myself that God is working everything together for our good.

Sometimes the frustration of things going slowly with the house sale and my husband's work situation made me lose motivation for GP work, but I kept going to work because there was work to be done. A 60-year-old patient's wife shouted at me on the phone this week for advising that her husband get a Covid-19 test with his dry cough. He was a Covid-19 high risk patient with asthma, so I gave him steroid tablets for the exacerbation, but encouraged him to get the Covid-19 test discussed in his last consultation. His wife took the phone from him after a ten-minute consultation, telling me that she did not want him going out for a Coronavirus test or anything else in this pandemic. He was not ill enough to need admission and they both understood that antibiotics are not helpful for viral infections, so I explained that they could book the Covid-19 test online or by phoning 119 like everyone else. Home testing kits were also available. She insisted he did not need it, and got upset when I politely explained that I could not stay longer on the call due to other patients waiting. As usual, I told them to contact us or call 999 if he got worse. I was sad to find out a week later that he deteriorated and died in hospital after they called 999 for an ambulance. The cause of death was sadly Covid-19.

I had decided to work through until half-term break next month, and have time off with the children then. I was also saving some annual leave in faith for moving house soon. Thankfully, my husband started to get some locum work which I was so grateful for. He does not do well sitting idly at home. Some men dream of having a rich wife or parents so they do not have to work, but my husband loves to put on a suit and go out to work, which is something else I love about him. Even though healthcare professions are generally well respected in society, they are actually a means of service to people. Service through healthcare is a calling for some, not just a job.

I would often listen to Christian worship songs in my car just to refocus on God before starting my day of GP consultations. There were also good songs on Coventry's

Radioplus. It was a shame I did not have DAB radio in my car for my favourite Premier Praise radio station, but it was also good these days to be able to catch the 9am news on Radio 4 because of my new school drop off times. Schools now had a staggered drop off system for children in all years to reduce Covid-19 spread at the school gates, which meant I was often not heading to work (after dropping the children off) till around 8.55am.

My GP surgery was flexible in letting me start work later now that schools had resumed, and we were back to some sort of normality. Patients were not waiting in the surgery for me, so I could phone them when I got there. It seemed that some of the Covid-19 changes to the way we work as GPs would be continued long term, because it was more efficient. I missed seeing patients face-to-face, but I felt this phone triage system was definitely safer overall.

Many large companies were also closing down offices, because they found they could manage with a majority of their staff working from home. Homebuyers were now keen for home offices and gardens, which I was glad our house had. There was really nothing uncomfortable about where we were. The house, school and neighbours were great. It was just time for change. As much as I wanted to hold out in faith for a buyer soon, I listened to my husband and mortgage adviser to move to a fixed-rate mortgage deal with our current lender while waiting. I was so glad we did, because we ended up with no viewings with this estate agent for the rest of September, and mortgage rates started to go up in the following months, as banks became more cautious in the pandemic.

I decided to visit another "outstanding" school close to our "dream house" in Stratford, so that I could widen our search area for a house. Schools in the UK are rated by Ofsted (the educational regulatory body) as outstanding, good, or "needs improvement". An outstanding school was usually the best choice on paper. I did not want to feel stranded if our dream house sold again. As much as I believed God would keep this house for us if it was meant to be ours, I also wanted to increase our options for when we eventually had a buyer and needed to move. Maybe our house had not sold because we hadn't yet seen the house that God wanted for us. Some friends also encouraged me by saying that the house we were going to buy was probably not even on the market yet. That made sense. New houses are added online every week, and people end up buying from whatever is available at the time of their house move. I prayed that God would continue to guide our steps. The fact that the outstanding school let me come in and look around in this climate seemed like a good sign. My friend's children were at that school, and she had so many good things to say about it, but I still felt that the other "good" school worked better for our family. I appreciated having options, in case another suitable house came up closer to this school than the other. I was also very happy when the lady told me that they had spaces in this year's Reception and Year 2, which was very unusual for an outstanding school like theirs. God always provides for His people, I thought. It will be interesting to see where we end up.

Meanwhile, in Nigeria, my parents were daily thanking God for His protection. There had been many political and religious killings in Kaduna state, where I grew up. We often pray for Nigeria, but most Nigerians really cannot see how things can improve. It really got to a peak in 2020 when people, including celebrities, started campaigning on social media to "Stop the killings in Southern Kaduna", where my parents are from. We would often get gory Whatsapp images and videos of massacres from close to where my parents lived. At some point I had to leave some Whatsapp groups, because the sad news was making me depressed and angry at the same time. It was really not news you wanted to wake up to every morning - yet some people lived in those situations. Why would God let these evil people continue to oppress harmless people? Why have there been no good leaders in all this time to turn things around? Some mornings, I would wake up with a very heavy heart and even struggle to go to work, but God's spirit kept reminding me that we can change things through prayer. I didn't even know what exactly to pray for. Jesus tells us to love our enemies and pray *for* them. It was so hard to know what to pray for people who kill your cousins and friends.

My brother in Nigeria was also planning to get married in December 2020. I was glad I met his fiancee last Christmas, but it was sad that we could not attend the wedding in Nigeria as planned. My parents planned to come to the UK after the wedding for Christmas, but they insisted that it was not safe for me to take the children to Nigeria in the current climate. I wondered if my brother would be able to have the usual big Nigerian wedding party parents normally throw. I guess the silver lining in that cloud will be the money saved. My husband and I had over 1,000 people at our Nigerian wedding ten years ago. Imagine getting all the presents without having to feed the crowd. Maybe couples this year should just send out wedding gift registry links with a Zoom wedding invitation: enjoy your own cake at home for us, but don't forget to buy a present. Maybe not.

We were in a routine again with swimming lessons for the children after school on Thursdays. News of a second wave of rising cases of Covid-19 was everywhere. Face masks were now compulsory for adults in our school and leisure centre. I even had a spare mask in my wallet, in case I forgot to take one out. Quite a few children did not return to swimming lessons when leisure centres initially reopened, and it looked like my children enjoyed the benefit of more attention from the swimming instructors with fewer students per class in lockdown. That was the reward for our bravery, I thought, hoping the absent children were all alright. You can imagine my pride when my boy was swimming ahead of the other two children in his little class for the first time ever. There was definitely significant improvement in his swimming skill and confidence this month, thanks to Coronavirus smaller classes. And who said black people can't swim?

On the way home, I could hear him chatting with his sister in the back of my car.

"Tell me about Harold."

"Oh ok. So Harold saw the doctor, and the doctor said, 'You have chicken pox.'"

"Aww" My son looked intently at his sister as if he was having a private stand up comedy performance.

"'Oh no!' Harold said, 'I don't want to be a chicken!'" She said in a funny baby voice.

My son burst out laughing, as she carried on with her funny stories about Harold, who I gathered was a new character she made up this week. This is something they started doing this month, when we banned TV on weekdays. After the overdose of TV during lockdown, I thought it would be a good idea to try and regain some creative play skills and have time for homework after school. The first week was painful for us all, because they kept coming to ask me what to do. My children love reading, but there was only so much of that they could do. A few weeks of extra TV time had got them using American accents and saying their toys were boring. I was impressed to see how quickly things changed. Now, they don't even miss TV because they are doing junk-modelling and making their own shows, which we sometimes get invited to watch as parents. The last show they set up for us in the lounge even had social distancing signs, so I had to sit 1m away from my husband, but the little actors still had American accents!

Our weeks seemed to be full again with swimming and music lessons after school. We left out gymnastics post-lockdown, but I signed them up for some extra maths and English lessons on Saturday mornings for 30 minutes every week, because I wanted to support the teacher's new business and felt bad about all their time off school this year. My daughter had lost some maths confidence and my son was still trying to accept the fact that he had to learn to read for himself. I decided to pay for two months only, and told the teacher we would not be able to commit to longer because we were planning to move house soon. I am so glad we did not sign up for longer, because the daily homework was definitely not right for our family in this season. Their dad took them to the classes on Saturday mornings when I was at work, and I encouraged them to do the daily exercises after school on weekdays, which helped to get them back into school mode.

After a few weeks, it became laborious trying to fit in time for homework every evening after school and other activities. There was hardly any time for the little homework they got from their own school, after playtime. I sometimes gave them two sheets on one day and skipped a few days. The tutor must have thought we were the most unserious parents when we brought back half-done work sometimes and asked for less work. I was not too bothered about pushing them this year as long as they were doing well and keeping school teachers happy. My daughter's maths confidence and ability greatly improved with a few weeks of daily practice, and my son was now keen to read and spell. Sometimes all you need is consistency and routine, so that there is no room for fear of school work to set in. Avoidance is how many people end up hating certain subjects without even trying. We had now achieved what we wanted for maths and English, but I did not want the children to think that they could quit things whenever it got hard, so we decided to stick with the Saturday classes and homework until the end of next month, as planned. I did not want my secret lack of love for maths to be inherited by my daughter, who also loves writing.

At the weekend, we decided to go for a walk by a water park with some friends from church, after the usual Sunday morning Zoom meeting. It was great to catch up in lovely September sunshine. The children enjoyed playing on the slides and having ice lollies, while the adults caught up on life. We thought it was a great meeting place, and planned to do it again, since it was somewhere I did not mind, as the least outdoor-loving one of the group. I had a complete change of heart by the next day after I could not sleep because of horrible itchy insect bites on the exposed areas of my arms and legs. I had a lot of patients call about insect bites this summer and always advised patients calmly to use antibiotics only if the bites were infected and to try Piriton from the pharmacy. After almost overdosing on Piriton and steroid cream just to get some relief from the horrible bites, I developed a newfound empathy for patients calling their GP about insect bites. Never mind Brexit and immigration, we need to sort out the evil small flying creatures in England!

We had another viewing, and the buyer seemed to be an investor buying houses for cash. He did not know much about our village, and I definitely did not think ours was the kind of house he would be hoping to buy cheap and resell. I sorted out my lovely showhome presentation for the viewing, but happened to be home while the agent was showing the man around. At this point, I was happy to let anyone look around the house, as long as they could buy it, so I could move. I did not realise how much I had invested emotionally into the renovation of this house, until he started talking about possibly tearing it down and building a duplex on the land. It felt like daggers in my heart when he said the layout was not great for his investment ideas, and they would at least have to tear down the kitchen. What?! Not my kitchen! Do you know how many different places I looked, compared prices and styles, researched brands and durability, to be able to come up with the best kitchen for us? I had to smile through it all, but couldn't wait to tell my husband about it at dinner. I love how my husband always knows how to bring me back to reality with just a single sentence: "What does it matter what he does with it, as long as he pays the right price so you can buy what you want now?" Painful, but true. I accepted that this was going to be someone's dream house or project soon, so I had better stop feeling so precious about it, but I was secretly happy the cash investor did not buy it in the end.

I kept getting letters from other estate agents in the post, asking if we wanted to try them since we had been on the market for months. Each one made me more annoyed about the situation with the current agent who had only managed two viewings in almost eight weeks. I decided to call a few other estate agents and started working on our multi-agent plan for when the current sole-agent contract runs out at the end of this month. One agent spent several minutes on the phone with me saying how much better their agency would be with communication and marketing the property. She even offered me a lower fee with no tie-in period, and booked a day to come and get photos of our house. I always had to do these estate agent meetings in my precious one hour between GP morning work and picking up the children from school. After all the hassle of getting the house ready for new photos and asking the children not to touch anything before we all left that morning, the estate agent did not turn up! I hardly got an apology when I called to find out why she did not come. I was just glad they showed their true colours now, before we signed up. Thankfully, I had another two estate agents coming that week, and they seemed much more professional.

Another estate agent agreed to come and see our house after hearing my frustrations about making no real progress since March. I wanted to salvage what time was left so we did not miss out on the stamp duty holiday. She told me that they were selling houses every week, even in our village, and that there must be something wrong with our marketing. I was pleased to see her, but by the time she left I felt properly whooped, as Americans say. She said we would need to repaint the house from top to bottom, change all carpets, get new cushions, new bedding, wash the drive etc etc. She also commented that the curtains and pillows did not sit straight in our current online photos and she felt that was enough to put some buyers off. She talked about how people paying this much for a house wanted the perfect home. I genuinely felt bad, because I had subconsciously switched off this house, not wanting to buy anything new until we got to our next house. Even the doormat needed changing, but I ignored it. After all, I had seen some terribly run-down houses sell, and I knew some buyers wanted to choose their own style and colours.

My husband wisely advised me not to go with that agent, because she would always have something more for me to do for the house if it took longer to sell. I was not about to spend thousands repainting and re-carpeting a house I was planning to move from. I did accept that some of the criticism was needed though. A new doormat, decor, cushions and bedding were things I could take with me to our next house, all of which could make this house more attractive to prospective buyers. I went out to do some retail therapy, killing two birds with one stone. I did restrain myself from buying my son a bigger bed though, because I believed it would be okay to wait for the next house for that one. It would be too much hassle to set up the bunk bed he wanted, only to take it down again for a house move. Our house felt nicer to live in with the little redecorating I did, so I thanked her again in my heart for motivating me to love where I am until I could go where I wanted to be. I even booked a professional cleaner, who did a fantastic one-off deep clean that got me loving my kitchen all over again.

Chapter 10
OCTOBER
Flu season

Almost three weeks after a phone call to request one, I was still waiting for a quote to clean our driveway. I found a driveway cleaning company online after one estate agent motivated me to improve our curb appeal. She was going to recommend someone, but could not find their number, so I half-heartedly called a number I found on google. They were meant to be one of the best driveway cleaning companies in the West Midlands. The man initially tried to dissuade me from cleaning the driveway this month, because "it was too early for the summer clean", then he asked if I could send him photos of my house for the quote because he could not come out. Talk about barriers to access. If someone called my company looking for a quote, I would try to make it easy for them to stay and work with me, not giving them excuses not to. It seemed like this one probably had too much work or did not need the money, but he eventually took our full address. He agreed to check out our driveway size on google streetview and get back to me with a quote for cleaning it.

Other tradesmen were still going out to work, so I was quite surprised at how uninterested he was. I guess it is better for tradesmen to show their true colours early, so you know not to book them, before they let you down after a date for the job is agreed. Or maybe I should have called one of the immigrants who come here to "steal our jobs".

I did not feel the need to chase this driveway cleaning idea anymore after this disappointment. Besides, the driveway man might have had more serious health or family issues he was dealing with in the pandemic. Who knows? It is always good to give people the benefit of doubt, especially in this difficult season, but better communication from him might have helped to keep my confidence in his company. He could have easily told me they were closed for now, if so. Anyway, we signed up with three estate agents initially on a multiagent contract after our sole agency contract finally ended last month - with no offers. It took that last estate agent several days to reply to my email confirming the contract end date, and a week after the contract end date to remove their horrid 'For Sale' board. It felt great not to have that board up anymore, but several friends assumed it meant we had now sold, so I had to keep explaining on school runs that we were yet to get a buyer. Some of the agents I contacted had very high fees for a multiagent contract, and explained why they felt they deserved a higher fee. I decided to sign up with one expensive agent and other regular ones. One particular young estate agent charged a lower fixed rate and seemed to be from a newer company, so I decided to give them the first chance at this, because I love supporting new businesses. They listed our property online at an agreed slightly lower sale price, and I was pleased to have five viewings with them in the first two weeks.

At least we were now getting more interest, and those who viewed were all proceedable buyers who wanted to view other properties before deciding. Things were looking up. I focused on my GP work, writing and everyday activities, so I would not drive myself crazy waiting for their feedback. Two potential buyers later said that they felt our garden was not long enough for them, which was fine. I also invited our first estate agent to take a multi-agent contract with us this time if interested, and they did. I was hopeful that having a few agents marketing the property would increase our chances of selling, but I was also trying not to seem too desperate online. My idea, whether it helped or not, was to re-list our house on different weeks with the agents, so that Rightmove notifications would be sent out to new prospective buyers every 10-14 days. I observed that only the young estate agent, who was very proactive with good communication, was getting us viewings. I felt that this proved my point that selling houses was not just about listing them online, and estate agents could be more proactive about selling. I guess all estate agents will have their own side of the story as to how much effort they put into marketing which house, but I just wanted results.

My dreaded GP appraisal date was finally here. I was not looking forward to having another appraisal after only just completing my GP training 10 months ago, but I felt prepared and wanted to get it out of the way now after weeks of anticipation. There were speculations that appraisals would be cancelled due to the pandemic this year, and even if they were not, I was meant to have mine next year; so you can imagine my surprise when all GPs got emails to say that we would be having appraisals this year. Mine was scheduled for October. I hate leaving things until the last minute, so I was already making entries in my GP career eportfolio for an appraisal next year, but it was nowhere near what I needed for a good appraisal now. I emailed last month to double-check that I too would be having an appraisal this early, and asked what I needed to prepare. There was so much going on with the house and work, that this felt like just another thing to worry about. Thankfully, I was told that the appraisal this year was mostly a wellbeing check on GPs in the pandemic, rather than a check on our eportfolio entries. My appraiser was very pleased with all I had achieved in the pandemic, including my audit. He seemed genuinely interested in my wellbeing, so I told him about our trying to move house. It was nice to see his good report in the end, which was encouraging for me as a newly qualified GP.

We got wider recognition as a GP surgery this year for the work we were doing in reducing opioid prescribing in our patient population. All those difficult consultations and verbal abuse seemed worth it when the numbers proved we were seeing a change in patient attitudes to opiods. Even though working in the health sector can often be a thankless job, it is fulfilling to be recognised for the difference we are making. Our nurses do a great job with smoking cessation programmes, weight loss advice, vaccination schedules, cervical smear tests, annual health checks for patients with diabetes, asthma, learning disabilities etc. Patients were not able to drop in thank you cards and chocolates as usual this year, but it made me laugh this week when one patient said, “Thank you Doctor, you have put me at bloody ease!”

GPs have to care for their own bodies too. I blamed it on the colder weather when I noticed that I was using the toilet more often at work for a couple of days. I had also been very tired during the weekend before and thought it was because of house chores. It started stinging whenever I urinated, and then the penny dropped when I used the toilet twice in one hour before work one morning. It is usually easier to make a diagnosis from a patient's history, but with my own body, it took almost four days for me to realise that I had a bladder infection. Thankfully my own GP was also doing phone consultations and sent me an electronic prescription on the same day after I phoned for antibiotics to clear the infection. I guess I was not drinking enough water and looking after myself with everything else going on. As someone who hardly gets ill, this was a wake-up call to start paying more attention to my own body, even in this pandemic. This is also the same reason why I encourage my family and friends to speak to their own GP, because it can be easy to miss diagnoses and changes in people you are familiar with. There was no sick leave for me. I worked from home one day and continued as normal the rest of the week while treating my bladder infection, which cleared up in three days with no complications - thank God. I have seen enough people end up with confusion and sepsis from a simple urinary tract infection like this to be grateful for such healing. Some people think that they have to choose either medication or prayer, but I believe in both. Not everyone who takes medicines gets better and I believe it is God who provides the healing and medical wisdom to treat. So yes, thank God antibiotics worked for me.

At work, I try to follow up on patients that I suspect can be easily forgotten because they do not ask for much. They are often so grateful for just a simple unexpected phone call from their GP. This week, I phoned a gentleman whose blood results showed signs of alcohol damage to his liver. It was an ongoing problem and there was actually nothing urgent. I spent ten minutes on the phone hearing about how he was now trying to stop drinking, but depression and loneliness often made him go back to the bottle. He explained how it was hard for him to ask for help and asked me what each blood test meant. After I explained and signposted him to some useful services to help him stop drinking safely and successfully, he thanked me saying that I had done more for him in ten minutes than anyone had in years. He also agreed to start some medication he was meant to be taking, and said he was happy for me to call anytime. I offered him a follow up appointment in two weeks to make sure he was getting the help he needed. It was interesting to see that a ten-minute phone call can mean so much in times of loneliness, but this is a way we all can help each other these days. The strength, laughter and wisdom we take for granted might be just what someone else needs from us in their lowest moments.

I sometimes feel guilty about not taking time to call my own parents and siblings as much as I would like. We chat most days on Whatsapp, but there is something better about hearing someone's voice and seeing their face on a video call, for example. My main excuse is the frustrating internet connection they sometimes have in Kaduna. You wake up excited to speak to your family, but get off the phone in a bad mood after saying 'Hello' fifty times to a frozen screen. Thankfully, it is getting better. My parents confirmed that they could come to England for Christmas, so I had that to look forward to. Even my children could not wait to see Grandma and Grandpa. It was a massive answered prayer to hear that the killings in Southern Kaduna had reduced because of the campaigns, but there was still national unrest in Nigeria this month because of corruption and police brutality. There was even violence during protests the people were now having with the #EndSARS campaign. Sadly, more lives were lost and more corruption was exposed in 2020.

God reminded me of how He raised Moses to save the Israelites from oppression in Egypt many years ago, and how he changed Saul, a persecutor of the church, into an apostle for Jesus to spread the gospel. Nothing is impossible with God. I found peace in being able to pray that God would change the hearts of corrupt leaders and raise brave, righteous leaders for Nigeria. As someone who is not into politics, it takes a lot to get my attention, and this was really something that needed to change. Sinach's *Waymaker* song was a great reminder for me that God makes a way where there seems to be no way. We are to be the light in the darkness, even when we worry that we might not be making enough of a difference. Foreign news like this also made me thankful for the peace and stability we enjoy in the UK, so I often prayed for more wisdom for our leaders here.

Work was getting busier again with parents worrying about common colds more than they normally would. I too found myself wishing my children would stifle their cough on the school grounds, because of the worried looks people had when anyone coughed during the pandemic. Even though there was no national lockdown this month, some areas of the country were put in local lockdown to reduce the spread of the virus. There was later a three-tier system of restrictions for England to put areas into medium, high or very high risk categories. Thankfully, there was good awareness of Coronavirus symptoms and more access to testing now, but anxiety was still high. Many patients I invited to the surgery for face-to-face appointments were children of parents who needed reassurance for the usual viral respiratory illnesses children get at this time of year. GPs still wore masks, gloves and aprons to be safe, and all patients over the age of five had to wear masks when visiting the surgery too. We also had to disinfect our offices and equipment after each face-to-face consultation, which made it a significantly longer session when I invited a few patients into surgery. The face-to-face consultations were probably longer also because some patients seemed to want to linger in my office when they finally got to see a doctor after such a long period of being limited to phone consultations.

I saw some extra cute babies this week. It was encouraging to see young mums in their postnatal checks coping well. People are actually more resilient than we sometimes give them credit for. It was a "new normal", but the news of rising rates of Coronavirus infection in the UK this month was concerning. I was thankful that we had no Covid-19 cases at our village school, so my children did not have to miss any school days this term. I had a cheeky "Thank God we have not moved yet!" face, when I read online that some children had to stay at home for two weeks at the Stratford school near our "dream house" due to Covid-19 cases. Interestingly, the classes affected were the two year groups my children would have joined if we had moved already. God always knows best. I prayed that the Stratford children were all okay with no serious symptoms. Like the good father that He is, God sometimes lets us see why He said no, though at other times He doesn't and we just have to trust Him. As much as I love spending time with my children, I am definitely grateful for not having to homeschool again this term so soon after resuming.

I met up with one of my lovely Christian friends in my precious one hour after work, and it was good to hear that they were doing well after resumption too. Some of her children had to stay at home due to Covid-19 cases in their classes, but her husband was able to help with childcare while working from home. Even though I joke about being lucky we never had Covid-19 cases in our little village school until now, I know that God would have given us the grace to deal with any issues that came up if we did. As someone who does not drink alcohol or coffee, there is no coffee fix before work for me, and no large glass of wine after a long day with the children. I just rely on Jesus, my rock. He is there for the good times and the bad times, so we have no fear of the future as God's people. He never fails.

We had a successful session of flu vaccination clinics at our surgery over two weekends to get patients ready for flu season. I hate needles myself, but I am quite comfortable with administering injections to patients. In fact, I have had kind compliments about my gentle hands from grateful patients. I was not thinking about needles when I came to work on this day in my sky blue shirt that reminds me of my final GP professional exam. It was the shirt I wore to London last year for my Clinical Skills Assessment, where examiners watched doctors in simulated GP consultations. I happily logged on to my computer at work and started phoning patients after a bit of paperwork, as I usually do. The senior GP partner popped in to say hi and said the words I had been dreading all week, "Can we all have our flu jabs today, please?" I took a moment to consider my options: run away and come back in March, lie that I have an allergy to flu jabs, or bribe the nurse to say I had already done it? None of them seemed like something Jesus would do, so I reluctantly got it done with very little dignity left after almost crying in front of the surgery staff because of a tiny vaccination needle. At least, I still looked professional in my blue shirt.

The days were getting colder and evenings were getting darker. I knew I would have to sort out my wardrobe soon, and stop waiting for a buyer before getting out the winter jumpers. I needed to wear tights with my dresses now, and it seemed like every pair I brought out of the wardrobe this morning had holes or ladders. This is so annoying when you are trying to rush out of the house for school and work. If it was not going to embarrass my fashion-conscious daughter, I probably would have just worn the torn tights and got out quicker. Thankfully, the fourth pair was okay. I need to remember to bin the torn tights, I thought - knowing my thrifty side would not let me do that. Torn tights are good for wearing under thin fabric trousers when proper winter comes. I still needed to buy some new tights though, before I drove myself crazy one more day being annoyed about holes in old tights.

We were in a good routine with school runs, and only needed the after-school club once a week for childcare when I was on call. Even though mums sometimes complain about having to do school runs, it is a huge blessing for me to be able to pick up my children after school myself most days now. I remember being upset about having to pass my little daughter from school, to the after-school club, and then to a babysitter before my husband got home at 7pm during my training years. All those sacrifices were worth it for the work-life-balance we enjoy now that I am a qualified GP. I just wished I could do something more to sort out the house move situation sooner. My daughter's teacher told me that she had been very possessive of her friends this term, not wanting them to play with anyone else. She put it down to little girls' squabbles, which often got sorted in a day, but I knew it had something to do with the fact that my daughter knew that she would be changing schools when we eventually moved house, and she was not sure when. This is why I thought it might have been easier to move in the summer to avoid this friendship separation anxiety, but I'm sure that God knows best. We just have to wait for His timing.

I wished we could have hidden our plans from the children, at least until we had a buyer. They were mostly happy in school, and I tried to reassure them that they would have playdates with friends from this village even after we moved, but we had a few tearful moments when they asked impatiently why God was not providing the new house yet. They looked forward to having new rooms and a new school, but they too had days of frustration at not knowing when it would happen. Proverbs 13.12 says: "Hope deferred makes the heart sick, but a dream fulfilled is a tree of life." Some days, I desperately wanted some good news to encourage us, but God sometimes wants us to learn to trust in His goodness, even when we do not understand. We had to carry our children along on this journey of faith, as our parents often did with us. My mother is still one of my greatest role models for unshakeable faith, like those listed in Hebrews 11. Being open and real about our feelings and faith helps children grow in faith, when they see that being a Christian is not about having a rosy life and every wish granted. It is really about following Jesus wherever the road leads us, knowing that He is good and will work everything out for our good. There are sometimes ungodly options and quicker shortcuts, but we chose to follow only God's leading through His Holy Spirit each day.

My four-year-old son had become quite passionate about sharing his love of Jesus with everyone. He made me stop to talk with a homeless man in Coventry on our way back from the library there one day. Even though the city centre was no longer quiet and deserted, it was sad to see restricted access to the library and people trying to smile at you behind their mandatory face masks. We all couldn't wait to see the back of this Covid-19 pandemic. People were dreading another lockdown if cases continued to rise, but the homeless man told me and my children that getting urgent accommodation from the council in the event of a lockdown was one good thing that came out of this for him. He was a young man with dreams like all of us. He asked us to pray that he would get housing soon and be able to work as a chef someday. We gave him what we could, and I told him about the gift that is worth more than money and houses - eternal life through Jesus. He said that he had heard of Jesus, but was not willing to make a commitment to follow God at the moment. I tried not to push it, but told him that Jesus accepts us all as we are, so he could always pray to God himself whenever he made up his mind. Jesus did not come to save perfect people, and my life would be empty without God. My little son cut through my polite explanation and said so cutely, "And you will go to hell, if you do not accept Jesus".

Moving swiftly on, I got the children home and fed them, so they could be in bed by 7.30pm, because we had a church life group meeting on Zoom, as usual on Tuesdays. We were reading Jarrod Cooper's book, *Stronger*, and I enjoyed the discussions. It was exactly what I needed this year - God's strength. When we try to do things in our own strength, we always fall short. The Holy Spirit is there to guide and comfort us, so it is best to rely on His power, even while working through a pandemic. I sometimes get frustrated about circumstances beyond my control because I am naturally a proactive and goal-setting type of person, but God has taught me so much this year about being flexible in following His plan, not mine. Being flexible does not mean jumping ship whenever there are challenges. We need wisdom to know when to stand still versus when to fight. Unsurprisingly, God also spoke to me through an episode of *Queen of the South*, an unusual series for me to watch on Netflix. I was heartbroken by what the main character had to live through while serving drug lords, but also impressed by her passion to succeed. If people are this passionate about doing what is wrong, how much more passionate should we be for the kingdom of God, our maker? In one episode, the main character's friend mentioned Psalm 144, which also became one of my prayers for 2020:

"May our sons in their youth
be like plants full grown,
our daughters like corner pillars,
cut for the building of a palace.
May our barns be filled
with produce of every kind;
may our sheep increase by thousands,
by tens of thousands in our fields,
and may our cattle be heavy with young.
May there be no breach in the walls, no exile,
and no cry of distress in our streets.
Happy are the people to whom such blessings fall;
happy are the people whose God is the Lord."

We stood on God's word even when we heard sad news of the UK unemployment rate going up, Covid-19 rates rising, domestic violence increasing and bereavements all around us. We had a guest speaker for some of our Zoom church meetings encouraging us this month to "hope in God". He shared how his hope in God saw him through his heart attack recovery and having a daughter with heart problems. These are difficulties I cannot even begin to imagine as a healthy person with well children. I could understand the part about hoping in God even when things did not make sense because of challenges I overcame in my past, by God's grace. This is more than positive thinking and positive confession. It is about experiencing God's powerful comfort through His Holy Spirit in us. It was indeed God's "peace that passes all understanding" (Philippians 4:7) which I experienced when the Stratford estate agent called this month to tell me that our "dream house" had sold again. I was not shaken, because I knew God will have something better for us, if not that one.

When I went to pick up my children from school on Thursday, I had to leave our house keys with our new young estate agent because he had another viewing booked. We arranged it for a time when I would normally take the children for their swimming lessons, so I had their swimming costumes in my car ready to drive there from school. I was running late to get my son from his Reception class, so I ran across the school field to get him before my daughter came out of her class. It was only after I got the children in my car that I realised I had lost my phone! It must have dropped out of my pocket when I ran. For those that do not have smartphones, you need to understand that losing a smartphone these days is probably worse than falling in a ditch. We rely on our phones too much!

I got my children out of the car and walked around the school searching for my phone to no avail. I put my car keys and wallet on the driver's seat when we got back to my car and decided to check on the floor of the car, with the children standing on the pavement. When I shut the driver's door to walk round and check on the passenger's side, the car strangely locked itself - with my key and wallet inside in full view! First, I could not drive off to swimming lessons without satellite navigation on my phone, now I had no car to drive. Yes, I use satellite navigation everywhere, and I should get a car with built-in navigation. I honestly felt like I was in a movie. What are the chances of both things happening to me on the same day?

I remained calm and thought of what to do next. Thankfully, my son's teacher was walking out of school with another parent, and asked if they could help. The phone signal in our village is quite poor, so their attempts to call my phone did not work. By some miracle, the other mum was able to get internet access on her phone to find my car breakdown cover provider's phone number, which I did not have because it was stored on my phone. The teacher also managed to get some phone signal for me to call them for breakdown support, which they said would be with me in 90 minutes! I did not have a watch to keep time or a phone for them to call me back on, so the kind ladies wrote down the breakdown cover number for me on my palm before they left, in case I needed it.

I suddenly remembered that there was someone viewing our house at that moment, and I could rush back to get the house key before the estate agent left, so we did not have to wait outside for over an hour in the autumn evening cold. Our house was only five minutes' walk from school, so we got back in time to catch the estate agent and collect our house key before he left. It was quite embarrassing to interrupt the viewing, but I was not about to stay stranded outside with tired children because my house keys were attached to my inaccessible car keys. I guess a neighbour might have taken us in if needed, but that would have been a less complicated request if we had not been in a pandemic. Thankfully, there was no need for that now with my house key available from the agent.

I had a chat with some lovely neighbours outside while waiting for the viewing to finish, and they could not believe how calm I was with all that was happening. I knew that God was in this mess with us and His peace felt so real. The children prayed with me for my phone to be found, and my daughter was beginning to get upset that their prayer was not answered. We were just about to go into the house when I saw a receptionist from their school running towards us with my phone! She said that someone handed it in and she was going to keep it in the drawer to return it to me in the morning, but decided to bring it since she knew our house. Thank God she did.

I was now able to phone the car breakdown service number to give them my contact details to let me know when the engineer was near. This was only 30 minutes after my first call to them, and they said he was actually on his way now. I rushed back to school with the children, and was pleased when he handed back my car keys which he removed from the car before we got there. Talk about excellent service. It was now too late for swimming lessons, so we decided to get some things from the supermarket and meet up with their cousin in Coventry, which made their day. My children were impressed to see how God answered our prayers and made a "bad day" better. I believe there must have been a reason for us to not be at swimming lessons on this particular day, because that was all we missed due to the crazy turn of events. When you live your life for Jesus, nothing happens by chance. He works it all out for your good - even the things the enemy meant for bad. If only we could see the big picture sometimes, we would be more patient with the troubles of life. God help us all to trust Him more. The following week, my son did very well at swimming and got moved up to the next stage.

We were excited to get to the last week of the month for a half-term break, and finally got an offer on our house! I was pleased to have an offer even if it was lower than we expected. The young estate agent said that he would negotiate with the cash buyer for a reasonable price while chasing feedback from the other viewers. I booked some fun days out for the children for half term week, while I was off work. We also decided to act on another idea to send letters to owners of similar houses near our sold "dream house" to see if anyone was considering moving soon to take advantage of the stamp duty holiday. There was only one other house on the market that I liked at this stage. It was exactly like our "dream house" but had a double garage, making it more expensive. My husband had also viewed and loved it. How wonderful would it be for God to give us a better house for the same price we were going to pay for the old "dream house"? I do know that nothing is impossible for God, but His ways are also higher than our ways. We decided not to make an offer for the double garage house until we agreed a sale on ours. Things were getting exciting, and I could not wait to see which house God would give us in the end. This walking with God and trusting Jesus business can be scary and exciting all at the same time. Thank God He gives us His strength for every day.

Ephesians 3.20-21
Now to him who is able to do immeasurably more than all we ask or imagine, according to his power that is at work within us, to him be glory in the church and in Christ Jesus throughout all generations, for ever and ever! Amen.

Chapter 11
NOVEMBER
Lockdown Two

I was pleased to have been able to visit Nickelodeon in London with my family in the half-term break before another national lockdown (from November 5) was announced. Thankfully, the government's furlough scheme and mortgage payment holidays were extended to help ease the financial impact of the pandemic on families. The stamp duty holiday which was the only one that concerned us was not extended, but I did not mind because house viewings and sales could continue in the second lockdown. It was a wet day in London for our Nickelodeon visit, but we had a nice drive and enjoyed the indoor activities. We also got to see my friend's new house, which gave me great ideas for our next house. With the Covid-19 restrictions, we felt so blessed to have been able to visit her, because she lived alone, making us less than six people altogether in the house. We missed the days when you could just visit anyone anywhere and hug whoever you wanted to. Even though we have relatives in London, we were not able to visit any couples who had children because that would have been breaking the "rule of six" which prohibited gatherings of more than six people, especially indoors. I had most of the half-term week off work, so I took the children to an outdoor showing of *The Greatest Showman*, which ended up being another wet experience. We had nice weather for a boat ride in Stratford and a long walk in Coombe Abbey park on other days with some friends from the Forte Charity Wazobia language classes. Even though the language classes were one of my big goals for 2020, I was not upset about having to end it early due to Covid-19, because I felt that we made some great connections and impact in the short time we had.

Our young and proactive estate agent called to let me know that he had another viewing for us, but it was disappointing to hear that the cash buyer who made the offer last month was not willing to offer any more for our house. I imagined I would have done the same, trying to get a good bargain as a cash buyer in a pandemic with so many economic uncertainties. It was encouraging to hear that the person coming to view this time was a first-time buyer, which would make things easier if they decided to buy. For me, it was also motivation to clean the house properly after a whole week of children's half-term play at home. Even our light brown lounge carpet was now red with markings from my son's drawing on the floor! I would normally get a professional carpet cleaner to clean the whole house every few months, but thanks to Coronavirus, this had not been done in a while. The unsightly red marks had to be sorted, so my husband used his precious day off to thoroughly wash all the carpets, making the house look great again - I almost forgot that I wanted to move.

I was not daunted by the thought of this second lockdown because house viewings and schools were allowed to continue, but I felt sorry for the many non-essential shops and businesses that had to close again for another four weeks. We were told that the lockdown would end on December 2, but plans for after that would depend on how controlled the virus spread was. Even though it was only four weeks, it actually felt worse than the first lockdown in the end. With the cold weather and shorter days, many people struggled in this second lockdown. I remember praying that there would be no need for another lockdown and trusting that God would make everything better by now, so I was slightly upset that the number of new cases was still going up, leading to another lockdown. I could already imagine how difficult this would be for the healthcare service, added to winter pressures.

Coronavirus results were often sent to patients' GPs, and we noticed in our own GP practice that the number of positive Covid-19 results had almost tripled this month. The numbers of new cases and deaths on the news kept rising. The UK had now passed the 50,000 mark for Coronavirus deaths. That's 50,000 human beings gone, 50,000 families bereaved, and God knows how many children left without fathers or mothers because of this virus. In my first week back at work after half-term, the receptionists told me about two of our registered patients who died of Covid-19 in hospital. I also heard that my dear uncle had a near-death experience in hospital with Covid-19 in Nigeria. Thank God he survived, but he shared how he had wished for death at times on admission because of how unwell he felt. I could see the despair in people's eyes at the mention of another lockdown. The anxiety and depression GP phone calls kept coming in.

While still trying to stay strong for the weeks ahead, I went on Rightmove and noticed that the double garage house that we liked had sold, and there was literally nothing else on the market that we wanted. Our young estate agent was unusually quiet after the viewing, so I texted him to know what was going on. He replied to say that the first time buyer made a low offer, which he knew we would not accept. My friend then told me how disappointed she was that the seller of the house they were trying to buy in Stratford had pulled out of the deal because his wife had just lost her job due to Covid-19 related cutbacks by companies. As it was the first week of lockdown2, I got an email, as expected, from my children's swimming school to say that swimming lessons would stop during lockdown. Although we might have been able to carry on with my son's drumming lessons, I decided to email his tutor to stop lessons until January too. This meant that we were now in lockdown2 mode as a family with nothing going on apart from key worker jobs and school. Thankfully my husband was still getting locum shifts, while waiting to start work at his own healthcare business when we got NHS England approval. It was so annoying that progress with this was also slow. I then got a message saying that my parents' December flight from Nigeria had been cancelled!

I was barely hanging on by a thread in my spirit after all these, when I went to put my children to bed one evening. We would normally read a Bible verse and talk about any good or bad things that happened that day. They both talked about their amazing friendships at school and how much they liked being at the village school. My daughter then told me how she now wanted to move house, but not school, because she did not want to miss her friends. I managed to smile through the rest of our time together and say 2 Timothy 1:7 with them, as we normally do: "*For God has not given us a spirit of fear, but of power, of love and a sound mind*" I kissed the children good night and met my husband in our room getting ready for a Zoom meeting we had. It was not the usual small group midweek meeting that night, but a whole church prayer and worship Zoom meeting, which I suddenly did not feel like joining.

At this point I was more than slightly upset with God. I felt like screaming. If only God had allowed us to sell and move to our "dream house" in the summer, we would not be dealing with children not wanting to change schools now, but I imagined it would be worse if we let them stay till the end of primary school. Besides, there was now no "dream house" and no other suitable Stratford house on the market. People were apparently pulling out of sales with job losses. The economy was getting more unpredictable with a second lockdown, leading to more low offers on our house. Patients I thought would make it had died, in spite of the fact that I pray for my patients. Coronavirus cases and deaths were rising, even after our prayers for Coventry and the UK as a church with Open Heaven in June, and weekly on the Sunday livestream. I was now hearing of Coronavirus cases closer to home, with close friends and family testing positive. I literally felt tired and depressed from all the bad news. I did not feel I could offer any more emotional support to people who had it worse than us. In fact, I know there will be people reading this and thinking how easy my 2020 was compared to theirs. There was only so much one could take of this pandemic. The disruptions to life and health were becoming unbearable. I was angry, and just did not feel like praying and praising God.

Even though my mind was angry and complaining, I decided to get into bed and log into the church Zoom meeting without video or sound, just to hear what was being said. As humans, we all have days when our strength fails, but that is not the time to run away from God. I knew that even if I did not feel like hearing about God in the midst of all this disappointment, that was really the best thing for me, especially now. Some people wander away from their faith for years, because of other choices in moments like this. I listened as people sang praises to God, while being quiet myself because I had nothing good to say. Slowly I felt God soften my heart and remind me of my immigration journey. How I came to England at 16 with hopes of becoming a medical doctor at 23. After years of delay, challenges and hardship, I eventually qualified as more than just a medical doctor at 28. God reminded me of the amazing things He did in and through me in that journey, showing me that He has a greater plan, even when we do not see it. Someone shared from my favourite Romans 8 verses and our church leader, who knew nothing about what I was feeling, read out this passage:

"So Jesus said to the twelve, "Do you want to go away as well?" Simon Peter answered him, "Lord, to whom shall we go? You have the words of eternal life " John 6:67-68

I do not remember anything else he said after that because I suddenly realised I had all I needed in Jesus, and this pandemic was not going to make me lose that. God can speak through anyone, when we choose to listen. I was still in our village for a reason, and our children will transition to their new school, with a sound mind as in 2 Timothy 1:7, at the right time. God is able to turn the disaster of this pandemic for good. This year did not only teach me patience, but also trust in God. I spoke with my husband and church friends about my feelings over the next few days, and thanked God for His love in drawing me near, even when I was ungrateful and complaining. I cannot possibly love people more than God our creator loves them. When we do not understand, and have no words to say, we can sing praise to God and trust that His promises will never fail. The song "Reckless love" by Cory Asbury still makes me want to cry when I think of how much God loves us, and draws us close with His kindness even in our childish murmurings.

"Oh, the overwhelming, never-ending, reckless love of God.
Oh, it chases me down, fights 'til I'm found, leaves the 99.
I couldn't earn it,
I don't deserve it, still you give yourself away.
Oh, the overwhelming, never-ending, reckless love of God."

Matthew 7:24 talks about building our lives on the solid foundation of God's word, so that when the storms of life come, we will still be standing. God has proven Himself faithful in keeping us through the storms of 2020. We later felt so blessed to still be in our village for lockdown2 because we were close to good friends in a difficult winter. We were able to support our neighbours who lost loved ones, and we also felt supported by them as a family on the tough days. It is good to see smiling familiar faces when you step out for work on cold mornings when you do not really feel like it. The short conversations across the road with neighbours opposite us meant more than usual in lockdown2. I finally gathered the strength to phone the airline about my parents' cancelled flights, and got the good news that it had been moved to an earlier date in December. My parents were so pleased about this because it was a better date, just after my brother's wedding in Nigeria. I realised that we sometimes work ourselves up, forgetting that things can change when we pray. I was not happy that the airline did not email to let them know about the earlier date, which they might have missed if I did not call, but I was happy that the flight cancellation email was really good news packaged as bad news. I wondered if my low offers for the house were also "good news packaged as bad news". We would look back next year and thank God that we did not move in 2020. I congratulate everyone who managed to move house in 2020 and hope that all works well, but the fact that we were able to decline those low offers peacefully made me realise that we were really not desperate for Stratford now. It is good to have done our research to know exactly what areas and houses we want there, so we can move with confidence when everything lines up, in God's time. As they say in Nigeria, delay is not denial.

I used the extra time in lockdown2 this month to sort out Forte Charity projects in Nigeria with the help of trustees there. So many families had been displaced in Southern Kaduna after the killings in small villages. We decided to pay for one year of better rented accommodation for five families with small children to help them settle down and go back to school. It was so touching to see videos of gratitude from the mothers, who were women like me wanting a good life for their children. We also approved some higher education tuition fee grants as usual to students who needed it when Nigerian universities resumed. The impact of a pandemic like this is most felt by people living in real poverty, and education is normally the first "luxury" to be dropped when things get tough. It was good to be able to help young people through Forte Charity to keep pursuing their academic dreams to build a better future for themselves and their families with good qualifications and jobs. Even though we were not able to do much fundraising this year for the charity, we were determined to make sure that the money raised went to people who really needed it. I really looked forward to seeing my parents in December, especially because of all the security issues in Nigeria. With the Coronavirus updates this month, I knew that flight schedules might change again, but I chose to trust that God will keep them safe and bring us together at the right time. It would be great to have a full house for Christmas with them here. My children were really looking forward to that. For someone like me who likes to stick to a plan, this year was very difficult to cope with in that way, but I am grateful for the more important things like good health and joy.

My mother spent some weeks in Lagos with my sister who was pregnant with her first baby. My sister was the ideal Nigerian daughter, having her baby in her first year of marriage, unlike us who waited years - enjoying a prolonged honeymoon! It was nice to finally have some good news when she gave birth to her baby boy without any complications. Knowing my sister's medical history, I knew that was a miracle and my heart rejoiced greatly in God for answered prayers. We saw lots of pictures and videos, which had to suffice in the pandemic. We looked forward to being able to cuddle him when travel was no longer restricted or unsafe. From what I was hearing, Coronavirus was no longer at the forefront of people's minds in Nigeria as it was here, because of the more worrying security issues and protests. I just prayed that God would keep my little nephew safe from infection.

So many people turned to God in prayer this year for their health and that of loved ones. I hope that we would not all go back to taking God and life for granted when all is well. I never knew there could be a time when money could not help and visas did not matter. Wealthy Nigerians who wanted to travel abroad to the best hospitals in the world could not travel. Celebrities who had money to pay for the best restaurants and hotels all had to stay at home like the rest of us. It was good to have the internet as an outlet to the outside world, but imagine a lockdown in places where there was no electricity or internet. You really only had God to turn to at times in 2020. Even family and friends had to stay away from each other to reduce the spread of Coronavirus. Hospitals were worried about the lack of intensive care beds and capacity to care for seriously ill patients. Our usual coping mechanisms and comforts had to change. No more retail therapy. Going to church once a week for a pick-me-up was not an option. You needed real resilience to work as a doctor, and you really had to have a personal relationship with God to see you through as a Christian this year. I kind of got used to Zoom meetings and communion with Christian friends on the screen, but some sadly withdrew to a lonely, vulnerable place in lockdown. I pray that God's reckless love finds them too.

This month, it was exciting to hear news of Coronavirus vaccines which were 70-95% effective and likely to be available from next month. We had just begun to catch our breath as GPs after flu vaccinations for this winter, and knew that the Coronavirus vaccination scheme would be mostly a job for GPs. It was interesting that the vaccine was likely to need storage at very low temperatures and patients would need two shots, weeks apart. As a new drug, we would also have to monitor patients for at least 15 minutes after injections for any allergic reactions, and we knew that some side effects were yet to be seen.

This was going to be a big challenge for the healthcare system but we were confident it could be done, especially if that is what is needed to build the herd immunity to conquer this pandemic. Many people welcomed the news of a Coronavirus vaccine, while others worried about the contents and possible side effects of a new vaccine. I decided not to worry about what was not yet approved by regulators. Scientists were working hard and GPs were preparing in advance, but we were yet to have confirmation of approval for the vaccinations in the UK.

There was also good news about the UK economy improving over the summer after the first lockdown, but there were worries about the effect of the second lockdown and after-effects of the UK government's stamp duty holiday and furlough schemes. There were speculations of house prices dropping next year and low availability of mortgage products. I was not worried about all this because I knew that God would look after us, no matter what. I just hoped that the negative news would not have a worse impact on people's mental health in lockdown2.

NHS England finally came through with the approval for my husband's healthcare business, and things started moving forward again in that area. Official processes were taking longer than expected because of the pandemic, but I was now very happy with NHS England for their positive response. It was very exciting to see another dream come true for us in 2020, in spite of the challenges. We decided to take our house off the market at the end of this month and focus on setting up the business after enjoying Christmas. With our experience from this year, I now know which estate agents to avoid if we decide to go back on the market next year. I still believe that proactive marketing gets results, because we could have moved if we accepted any of the lower offers we got this year. I also found out that many people with the "SOLD" signs that taunted me actually accepted offers that were significantly lower than the asking price for their houses. I read on the news about people losing thousands of pounds when homebuyers sadly pulled out of deals this year for pandemic-related reasons, and I was very grateful that God spared me such heartache and we did not lose any money.

The less productive agents on my multi-agent house selling plan were asked to remove their listings for our house on Rightmove. I did not want to waste any more time on this issue. The most expensive estate agent finally got us two viewings this month. The first one sounded positive, but never came back with an offer. I wondered if someone might knock on our door with a good offer after we took it off the market. The second viewing was cancelled because the potential buyer unfortunately had to go into hospital on the day of the viewing. I really hoped it was not something serious, or Coronavirus for that matter. We prayed for him as a family that evening, and I genuinely did not feel desperate for the viewings this month. I was also not as obsessive about keeping the house tidy all the time in lockdown2, so the viewing appointment really just gave me motivation to declutter the house and finally remove outgrown clothes from the children's wardrobes.

It was nice to still have school and work to go to this time, so we did not have to be indoors all the time. It made my day at work to see a teenage patient who remembered seeing me in January (he had a sports injury, which was now better). January felt so long ago. It had been over 11 months since I started this GP job, before the first lockdown. I imagined there would have been many more of such repeat face-to-face patients, if we did not have so many phone consultations this year, but we were all doing our best considering the circumstances. As it says in Esther 4, perhaps I became a UK GP (with a special interest in mental health) "for such a time as this".

Thankfully, Personal Protective Equipment (PPE) for healthcare workers was in good supply now. I remember how members of the public kindly volunteered their sewing skills earlier this year to make masks and scrubs for workers during times of shortages. I spoke with some stressed hospital colleagues this month and hoped for all our sakes that the second lockdown would really achieve the aim of reducing Coronavirus infection rates, so we can all have a good Christmas. The police had to give fines in 2020 to people breaking Coronavirus rules, such as isolation or not wearing masks. One woman complained in the media about how a fine of £6,000 which she got for going out when she should have been isolating, led to her losing her job and friends. The police must have had a hard time with some people refusing to follow Coronavirus social distancing rules around gathering in public places, especially when pubs reopened in the summer. It must have been a difficult time for people in the armed forces too with all the news about police brutality in Nigeria and America. I just hoped that they too were getting pastoral support from their organisations. It is so sad when a few bad people make things difficult for the majority who are there to serve. Other unsung heroes of 2020 are the administrative staff who kept things moving even in lockdown. Over 100,000 patients at this point were waiting for NHS procedures delayed because of

Covid-19. Some who had operations cancelled or postponed were taking out their frustrations on us via telephone GP consultations. I could only imagine the pressure on the NHS administrative staff managing the clinics and surgical appointments for our large hospitals and busy consultants. GP receptionists and secretaries also had their fair share of Covid-19 stress with the seeming lack of GP appointments with rising demand in a pandemic. They all showed great resilience over the months, which we truly appreciate.

Even though I was happy that schools stayed open for lockdown2, I could imagine the stress on teachers and school workers, especially where there were Covid-19 cases in schools. We all knew that this lockdown could not be as effective as the first lockdown with schools staying open, but we hoped for some impact. Roads were not as quiet this time, and it was easier to pop into supermarkets because Covid-19 measures were already in place. We used to have to queue at the supermarket entrance to wait for staff to invite us in when people come out, so there would not be too many people in the store at once. This time, some stores had a light on the door that turned green if you could come in and red if you had to wait. There were still markings on floors of public places reminding us to stay 2m apart, and there were one way systems to keep safe flow of pedestrian traffic.

The reality of high numbers of Covid-19 cases in Coventry and Warwickshire hit close to home for me when my close friend's husband, who is a teacher, tested positive for Covid-19. Thankfully, the rest of her family remained well, and her husband did not need hospital admission. With so much going on and many people having to work from home again this month, it was interesting to see some early Christmas decorations around. Some people put Christmas decorations up in their houses from the start of lockdown2 to keep their spirits up, and shared photos on social media. We also saw decorations and lights outside some houses in our village from mid-November, which was about three weeks earlier than usual. Not much changed for us as a family with school children in lockdown2, so we saved our Christmas decorations until the first week of December, as we normally do. I was finally looking forward to Christmas in our lovely village, after accepting that we would not be moving house in 2020.

Chapter 12
DECEMBER
A Different Christmas

In spite of the work ahead of us as GPs with winter pressures and possible Covid-19 vaccinations, I felt very peaceful in December, the month of Christmas. I had to cover a few on-call shifts for my GP colleague who was moving house and I did it gladly, with no jealousy at all. Even my "Rightmove addiction" had been cured, because I was back to looking at photos of my children and nephew between patients when I needed a mental break. I guess it was easier to forget Rightmove when there was literally no house on the market that I wanted. I did look a few times at some interesting floor plans and possible improvements I would make if I bought those, but I knew God could still bring back the double garage house as he did with the "dream house" or provide a better house for us, so I really was not worried about houses this month. Who knows? One of our direct letters to detached houses near the Stratford school might even lead to a good sale without estate agents next year. Nothing is impossible with God. I knew He could cause the government to extend the stamp duty holiday or provide the money for us to pay it if we missed the offer. God is so great He can even provide money for us to buy a bigger house without having to sell this one. He really can do anything!

My children's teachers had all good things to say about them at the Zoom parent-teacher meeting we had for each of them last month. They were doing great with their learning and friendships. Even my son was reading whole (small) books already! I felt so blessed that we had no absences, no school closures and no need for isolation as a family. When I heard of people who had more than three two-week periods of isolation this year, I knew this was a great blessing to be counted. Our school and village community had really pulled together to stay safe and do our best for the children, in spite of the challenges of 2020. Masks were still mandatory on school grounds, and the caretaker would even give parents masks to wear if they forgot to bring one. By December, we really didn't mind wearing the masks because they kept our faces warm in the winter. It was just such a waste though that no one could see all the nice shades of lipstick on women who still bothered to wear makeup this year.

I love suburban living. I was impressed by how much location mattered to me now after much research this year, that even the nicest houses in the wrong location for our preferred school and neighbourhood did not tempt me. No one knows what the neighbours are really like until you move into a house. This was one aspect I had to completely trust God with for our next house, because we have always had great neighbours while following God's leading for all our previous homes. I did not want to leave a nice neighbourhood to end up with neighbours from hell. I still wanted a bigger house closer to our new business, but I felt happier to wait. In the grand scheme of things, even another year is not too long to wait for such a big change, but no one could have told me this before now without God helping me to accept it.

I am sure that our journey with estate agents in 2020 had a purpose. Some of the estate agent contacts we made might come in handy for my property investments in future, or I might just have gone through it all so that someone going through a tough time this year could read my lovely wall decal during a house viewing. John 14:1 on our bedroom wall reminds me everyday of the words of Jesus: "Do not let your hearts be troubled, trust in God". We trust God to provide our new house when moving would not be too stressful for our family or business. When God gives us dreams and desires, they do not come with a "Best Before" date. Joseph in the Bible knew for years that he would be prince over his brothers, but he was a slave and prisoner for years before that. Abraham knew for years that he would be a "Father of many nations", but Ishmael was the result of Sarah and her maid trying to help. We must not lose focus on God's word to us while waiting, but it is important to know by God's Holy Spirit when to push and when to wait. It felt okay to do nothing about this new house matter with our house off the market this month. We chose to just enjoy our beautiful home and good health.

I have been enjoying *The Queen's Gambit* for Netflix entertainment since last month. It is always fascinating to see how much things have changed for women over the years, but also interesting to see that some things have remained the same. The bondage of addiction has been around for generations, and sadly does the most damage in secret. I loved watching the main character in *The Queen's Gambit* succeed at chess, but the slow destruction of drugs and alcohol in her life was not as obvious to her admirers. It eventually took openness with and support from close friends to help her overcome this. Even in our day, many highly successful people rely secretly on drugs and alcohol to keep going. Thank God my head won't let me have any alcohol or coffee, so other drugs have no chance. As my Sunday school teacher used to say, there is a God-shaped hole in every heart. People try to fill it with all sorts of good and bad things - money, success, houses, alcohol, drugs, sex, family, hobbies, etc. I heard someone say that an idol is "anything we have to consult before we obey God". Any thing or person we depend on for satisfaction or happiness in life is really what we worship. As a Christian, God has the first place in my heart, even above my beloved husband and darling children. I have seen this year that He is truly worth it. Everything else will fail in the end, but God does not. His light can expose sin, addiction and other strongholds to bring true freedom, deliverance and hope when we let Him in. His love can reach us in the darkest pits when our loved ones have no words to say.

We had a few bereavements in our local church also in 2020, but interestingly none died from Covid-19. Some dear friends sadly lost their parents this year, and found it harder because they could not be with them (as they would have liked) in their last moments, due to the pandemic. Some were suffering with illnesses we had prayed about for years. We may never know why they were not healed on this side of eternity, but our joy is that they have eternal rest with Jesus now. In this same year, we have also seen supernatural healings and protection from deadly viruses as God promised in Psalm 91. It has really been a year of plenty. Our young people in university have stayed safe and well this year. The government arranged more Covid-19 testing to allow students to come home for Christmas safely. So many that were traumatised by the A level results disappointments and cancelled exams in the summer have come out stronger at the end of 2020. We have all learned important things about life this year that I hope we will not forget when the pandemic is over.

The UK Prime Minister announced a plan for stricter tiered restrictions in England for after lockdown2, but there would be an agreed short period of relaxed Covid-19 restrictions over Christmas week to allow families to enjoy time together. Christmas was definitely not cancelled. I was so happy for students at university who would be able to see their families this month. Imagine being in university with Coronavirus restrictions. I used to look forward to seeing my husband at university, before he became my boyfriend, at church programmes and student parties, which seemed to happen almost every weekend. Even without Coronavirus restrictions, you had to go out of your way to have a social life in university. I can imagine how difficult the social distancing rules and lack of social gatherings made things for students living away from home. We do not have a big student population at my practice, but I know that there were sadly more cases of depression and suicide this year among young people.

It is very easy to assume that young people are doing well especially when they refuse to open up about their mental health, but we can try to be more approachable to those around us, and proactive in showing them love. Some students complained on the news earlier this year about having no way to get food and supplies while isolating when they tested positive for Coronavirus. We later saw photos of them complaining about the kind of food delivered by the government, which made me think of the Israelites complaining about manna! As someone who likes to focus on what I have rather than what I don't, I would probably have been so grateful for the food money saved as a student in such circumstances. There were still take-away restaurants delivering for those who really did not want that food, and I remember from my hospital days that patients who felt well enough to complain about the quality of food should really be thanking God for improved health. Rising cases of Covid-19 at universities were a big concern in September, but it was good to see a decline in the overall number of UK Coronavirus cases after lockdown2.

As well as plans for the vaccine, there was good news about plans for a new Coronavirus testing laboratory in Warwickshire. Although availability of tests had improved since the last lockdown, I agreed that it would be good to have quicker turnaround times for Covid-19 tests. The laboratory would also provide thousands of jobs, which can only be a good thing with the unemployment figures. As more Covid-19 tests were being carried out, we had more registered patients in GP that had tested positive. One such patient of mine also had Bipolar Affective Disorder, and was isolating with mild symptoms. She called us to request a referral to the mental health team because she had thankfully recognised a decline in her mental health during lockdown2 and wanted help. As a GP with psychiatry experience, I was able to review her medication and provide regular follow up before the psychiatrist's review of her manic symptoms, which she had previously needed admission for. She had good insight and knew that it would be complicated if she ended up needing psychiatry admission with Covid-19, so she agreed to increase her antipsychotic dose as I advised. Mental health teams were great at liaising with GPs and preventing so many admissions this year.

Even though it was a tough year, some of my friends started new jobs which God provided miraculously in the pandemic. One Christian doctor even launched an app for providing easier access to counselling for those with mental health problems. While some complained all year about the challenges, some people saw opportunities and made a difference to their world. While some focused so much on how hard things were for them, others thought about how to make things easier for people. I am sure that some reading this have sadly had a 2020 much worse than we can imagine, but I hope that they too can remain hopeful for the future because even Job, who lost everything, still hoped in God (Job 13:15) and smiled in the end. The God who is able to restore "years that locusts have eaten" (as in Joel 2:25) can surely restore what was lost this year when we trust and obey Him.

It is amazing that as we look away from our own problems and see the bigger picture, we find that we can be the solution to someone else's problems, thereby helping ourselves too. We soon realise that our problems are not as big as we think. We also see that there is nothing new under the sun, as it says in Ecclesiastes 1:9. Those feelings of anger, depression, loneliness, grief, helplessness, addiction, anxiety and insecurity are more common than we think. If we open up and talk about it with a good attitude to trusted friends, family or professionals who can help, we will find that someone else has experienced it before and can help us on our journey, so that we too can help someone else in future because of our own experience.

The Duchess of Sussex, Meghan Markle, talked in November 2020 about her "unbearable grief" with a miscarriage she sadly had in July this year. Having faith does not mean that we feel nothing. If anything, we feel it more because our hearts have been touched by a loving God who we know can do anything. We just choose to trust His love in every situation. Sometimes we need time to process our feelings and pain, while allowing His healing power to work in us, and that is okay. I was pleased to hear good news of marriages restored and married couples reconciled this month after the trials of 2020, but none of them happened by chance. Someone in each of the restored marriages chose to speak out, get help, pray, change, apologise and/or forgive. Trusting in God does not mean doing nothing and hoping everything gets sorted. Sometimes, it can mean sacrificing things like pride, laziness and selfishness. While my husband waited to start his own business this year, God did not provide another long term contract. We had to trust Him to provide work each week for four months, and He never failed us. Sometimes, my husband had to take lower pay rates or shifts in far places, but we were always grateful for God's provision and protection, believing that my husband has learned plenty from his recent varied work experience for our new business and future.

As we look forward to the years after 2020, some people expect things to get worse before they get better. Some expect that things can only get better. Some have lost all hope and motivation, waiting for life to happen to them as it pleases. We have really not seen the full impact of this pandemic yet, but I am very pleased at the news of an effective vaccine for Covid-19, which will be made available when approved, firstly to care home residents and staff, who have been severely hit by the pandemic. I am grateful for the dreams fulfilled and apparent disappointments of 2020. I am choosing to trust that God is working it all out for our good. Even if the only thing that came out of my "House for Sale" journey is this book, I hope that it has encouraged and inspired you somehow. I know that writing it has definitely helped me to grow in faith. I am choosing to believe that the lives of people lost in 2020 have not been in vain. The loved ones they have left behind will carry on their legacy and find comfort in the coming months to enjoy life again. Yes, life will never be the same again after all that has happened, but we can choose to accept change and move on to greater things, in spite of the challenges.

Christmas 2020, no matter what rules or relaxation of rules are in place, will be a very different Christmas, as I conclude this book a few weeks before the holidays. There will be no crowding in Santa's grotto or pantomimes in packed theatres. It will be the first Christmas without some Grandmas, Grandpas, Mums, Dads, brothers or sisters. It will be the first Christmas apart for some families, but it might end up being the first Christmas together for some, because 2020 has taught us to appreciate life, health and one another. We will no longer complain about long flights when we are finally allowed to fly freely and visit relatives abroad. People will finally be able to let go of grudges and enjoy being alive together after such a difficult year. People will write cards with meaningful words this year because they have had time to really talk or miss each other. People will truly appreciate having a warm house and good food, because so many jobs were threatened/lost and there were times of real scarcity in 2020. People will go out of their way to buy presents from and support small businesses who are still standing after two lockdowns. Children will have learned much more than what is taught in school, because of time at home with their own parents in 2020. Some will be having a new start because of significant changes to their home life and freedom from abusive relationships. We will make more sensible financial and travel plans for the years ahead because we will have realised that we do not always need expensive things to be happy. There is so much to appreciate at home, and we can be investing time and money to make home a happier place.

Do not be afraid to make plans and have goals for the future after the disappointments of 2020. The setbacks of this year should not become setbacks for life. I choose to focus on what we gained rather than what we lost. In a year like 2020, my extended family has grown with a little nephew and a new sister-in-law, and I know many people can say the same. One of our dear friends had a great-grandchild added to her family this year. We have learned to listen and care for our communities again in lockdown. We were able to celebrate our children's birthdays, even without the big parties. We can hope for a better summer next year, knowing that even if it was another lockdown instead of freedom from masks, God will give us strength again to get through it because His mercies are new every morning, as the Bible says. Hebrews 11:6 says that "Without faith it is impossible to please God, because anyone who comes to Him must believe that He exists and that He rewards those who earnestly seek him.". When our faith is in God, we can leave the timings to Him too.

Professionals and key workers will be working through the holidays, as they did in lockdown and previous Christmas holidays. They too might take a few days off this month to appreciate all they have been through in 2020, and spend time with family if they can. We will be more inclined to look out for lonely people who have no one to celebrate Christmas with this year. Millions of UK residents came to their doorsteps in lockdown to applaud NHS staff and carers every Thursday evening at 8pm from March 26 to May 28 this year. Even though no one is clapping for the NHS on Thursday nights anymore, we hope that the hard work and sacrifices of scientists, healthcare professionals and all key workers this year will never be forgotten. I hope that rainbows will always remind us that we lived through 2020 by God's grace. The prayers said by everyone around the world this year will continue to bear fruit and keep us strong for the days ahead, but here is a final prayer for us all in this book from Psalm 20 for the years after 2020.

Psalm 20 (Holy Bible, NIV)

May the Lord answer you when you are in distress;
may the name of the God of Jacob protect you.
May he send you help from the sanctuary
and grant you support from Zion.
May he remember all your sacrifices

and accept your burnt offerings.
May he give you the desire of your heart
and make all your plans succeed.
May we shout for joy over your victory
and lift up our banners in the name of our God.
May the Lord grant all your requests.
Now this I know:
The Lord gives victory to his anointed.
He answers him from his heavenly sanctuary
with the victorious power of his right hand.
Some trust in chariots and some in horses,
but we trust in the name of the Lord our God.
They are brought to their knees and fall,
but we rise up and stand firm.
Lord, give victory to the king!
Answer us when we call!
#PsalmPlenty

Other books by Afiniki Akanet

- Fortitude (The Story of a Nigerian Girl in the UK)
- Felicity
- Life Without Coffee (Choosing Happiness Over Stress)
- Taking CSA Tomorrow (Get in the right mindset for your MRCGP exam)
- Money and Mental Wellbeing

All available from **Amazon.co.uk** and **Afiniki.co.uk**